SUCCESS WITH

CACTI
AND OTHER SUCCULENTS

SUCCESS WITH
CACTI
AND OTHER SUCCULENTS

Shirley-Anne Bell

GUILD OF MASTER CRAFTSMAN
PUBLICATIONS LIMITED

First published 2005 by
Guild of Master Craftsman Publications Ltd,
Castle Place, 166 High Street, Lewes,
East Sussex, BN7 1XN

Text and illustrations © Shirley-Anne Bell 2005
Photographs © Neville and Shirley-Anne Bell
© in the work GMC Publications 2005

ISBN 1 86108 402 1

A catalogue record of this book is available from the British Library.

Production Manager: Hilary MacCallum
Managing Editor: Gerrie Purcell
Project Editor: Dominique Page

Designed by Andy Harrison
Set in Futura

Colour origination by Altaimage Ltd.
Printed and bound by Kyodo Printing, Singapore

Acknowledgements

Special thanks to my editor Dominique Page for all the hard work she has done on this book, to designer Andy Harrison, and of course to my husband Neville for all his photography and for his help and advice with the plant information.

Grateful acknowledgements to all those people who have so kindly allowed us to take photographs in their houses, conservatories, and gardens. Particular thanks to Mr and Mrs R Oliver, Swineshead, Lincolnshire for permission to feature their exotic garden scheme on pages 33 and 34 as well as plants in their home, to Mr Peter Freeland of Sussex for showing us his exciting cliff garden pictured on page 53, to Mr R Smy of Peterborough for allowing us to feature his garden on pages 13 and 38, and to Exeter University for allowing us to feature the innovative gardens on page 39. Grateful thanks also to Mrs M Day, Fishtoft, Boston, Lincolnshire, Mr B Leggott, Boston, Lincolnshire, Mr I Roberts, Benington Ings, Boston, Lincolnshire, and to Mr and Mrs T Wilson of Plant Lovers Nursery, Candlesby, Lincolnshire, to Baytree Garden Centre, Spalding, Lincolnshire, and to BGI Conservatories, Birch Grove Garden Centre, Spalding, Lincolnshire.

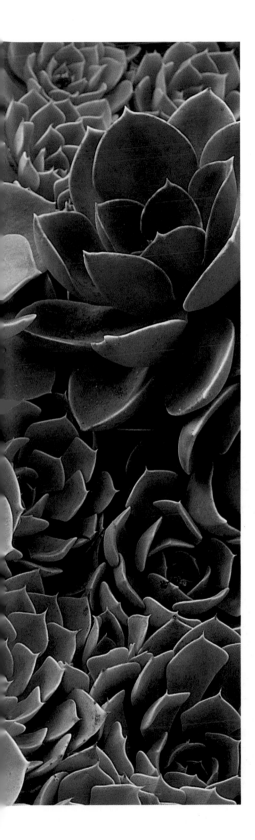

Contents

Introduction

No matter how large or small your space, from the tiniest windowsill to a deep bay window or a huge conservatory, there are cacti and other succulents for an unusual display in every part of the conservatory and the home. They also lend themselves well to interesting garden displays, where they can complement all sorts of hard landscaping and create displays with a contemporary feel. The scale of planting can range from striking plants in containers around patios to a total, uncompromising garden makeover.

In the home, ordinary houseplants have a tendency to parch in a centrally heated house, while a conservatory can be too hot during the summer months and too cold in the winter. However, cacti and other succulents are not only arresting and colourful but they suit a hectic lifestyle, tolerating far more neglect than the more commonly grown indoor plants. They will flourish on the hot and sunny windowsills and in porches and conservatories where other plants would suffer and perhaps die. They will also tolerate the cold temperatures of an unheated conservatory, so long as they are kept dry over winter.

In the garden, cacti and other succulents are striking and easy to care for and will tolerate the hottest and driest summers with no need for endless watering. They also associate well with a whole range of other dramatic architectural plants, and will grow happily alongside palms, phormiums, bamboos, ornamental grasses and other spiky subjects to create a really dramatic and unusual garden.

LEFT This conservatory rockery has a mini waterfall running through a mixed planting of echeverias, aloes, cotyledons and other colourful succulents

CHAPTER 1

What are succulents?

This book emphasizes the use and display of cacti and other succulents rather than their botanical detail, but it is important to explain the features which make these fascinating plants a homogenous group. First of all a definition: all cacti are classifed as succulents, but not all succulents are cacti. For convenience, therefore, I will refer to them throughout this book as cacti and 'other succulents'.

Succulence in plants is usually an adaptation to periods of prolonged drought and conditions of extreme heat. Plants in this situation need to slow down transpiration, the process through

ABOVE **From gigantic to minuscule, from prickly to hairy and fleshy, this family contains an amazing variety of distinctive plants**

which water is lost from the tissues. As a result, many succulents have a reduced surface area to avoid water loss as well as highly developed adaptations for storing what little moisture there is. Water can be stored in leaves, stems or roots.

In stem succulents, the stems are green because they have, to a larger or smaller extent, taken over the function of leaves and contain chlorophyll. Cacti are the best known of the stem succulent plants. They have adapted in the most

extreme way, in that their shape has simplified, with the stem becoming a water-storing sphere or column with a covering of thick wool or spines evolved from leaves, for protection from the heat and from grazing animals. The spines

RIGHT **A sheltered southwest-facing garden with windbreaks on either side and a back wall to retain the sun's warmth offers protection**

LEFT **These plants will thrive on benign neglect**

ABOVE *Trichocereus candicans* — a columnar cactus, with a thick covering of spines which have evolved from leaves

grow from the distinctive areoles. They often have ribs and tubercles, while others are smooth; their shapes are geometrical, forming columns and spheres.

The so-called 'other succulents', i.e. anything which is succulent other than cacti, have various protective stratagems to deal with the stresses of drought and excessive heat. The stem succulents among them are distinguishable because they have fleshy ribbed or jointed stems, often with tubercles, and any leaves are vestigial if present at all. Among some of the leaf succulents, such as lithops and some other 'living stones', the leaves have become simplified into a fissured pair of pebble-like structures, hence their name. In other cases, they have developed tight, interlocking, overlapping structures, forming columns or rosettes, or their leaves have become thickened with a glossy, water-retentive surface, or they have developed a soft, reflective, lightly coloured down.

The members of the final group are known as the caudiciforms. These are the real curiosities among what is already a very distinctive group of plant species. They have a hugely swollen caudex at the base of the plant, which is either an engorged root, an engorged section of stem, or a combination of the two. These plants often produce interesting twining and flowering stems.

LEFT The leaves of *Aloe gariepensis* have developed a thick protective surface to conserve water

ABOVE Lithops have pebble-like leaves for camouflage from grazing animals and maximum water storage

ABOVE *Dioscorea elephantipes* with its caudex, a water-storing organ that enables the plant to survive long periods of drought

ABOVE *Echeveria setosa* has a pale reflective down on the leaves for protection from the sun

The advantage of this adaptation to their surroundings is that most are easy to care for. Not only are they drought resistant, they will also tolerate strong sunlight, giving great flexibility, in that you can water and feed your plants when you choose to, rather than when you have to. They can be left when you go away and you can relax after a busy day, instead of needing to work on your plants – and therefore you can enjoy them instead of worrying about them.

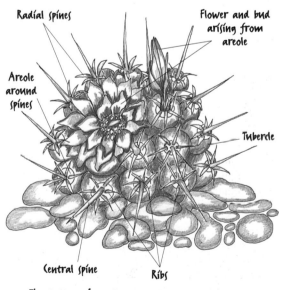

ABOVE The structure of a cactus

15

CHAPTER 2

Indoor displays

There is endless scope for using cacti and other succulents in attractive pots and containers in the house and in the conservatory. Displays are long-lasting and colourful, and they offer the advantage of portability, so that you can ring the changes. When a container looks at its best, perhaps with a lovely mass of flowers, you can feature it prominently before moving it into a less conspicuous position afterwards.

WINDOWSILL COLLECTIONS

Many homes have south-facing windows which are hostile to ordinary plants but which can look

ABOVE **The architectural shapes of the 'other succulents', such as** *Sedum nussbaumerianum* **(left) and** *Dudleya antonyi* **(right), can complement attractive containers to create spectacular indoor displays**

ABOVE **A windowsill comes to life with a colourful array of succulents**

very barren without any pots on display. Even in the most uncompromising positions, however, cacti and sun-loving succulents, such as the living stones, will flourish happily, delighting you with regular displays of flowers each year.

A normal windowsill will hold a range of small plants in pots and interesting containers, or can feature a row of spiny monsters. You can also add a second level of trailing plants, attached to hooks that are screwed into the top of the window recess.

A deep windowsill gives an increased scope for massed planting. It enables you to use accent plants, trailing or hanging subjects and a wide range of heights and shapes of cacti and other succulents. Using a table or shelf unit against the window can also provide additional display

RIGHT **Cacti and other succulents enjoy sunny positions which would scorch many other plants**

ABOVE Compact specimens are ideal for miniaturist table-top displays, contrasting vividly with spreading plants, such as the magnificent *Agave americana* 'Variegata' (left) with its variegated leaves

OTHER CONSERVATORIES

Other conservatories, like lean-to structures and off-the-peg add-ons, function as external rooms, which are halfway houses between indoors and outdoors, garden room and greenhouse. They will often have no blinds or curtains, and they may be equipped with more durable, patio-style furnishings and brushable concrete floors to withstand water spillages. In these structures it is possible to introduce a much more plant-orientated display, with raised areas, further beds in the ground and massed displays that can be watered with less fear of damage.

In conservatories such as this, think of your display as a painting, with a foreground, middle ground and background. Ideally you are hoping to strike a balance by using a variety of plants, with differences in height, shape, colour and size. Do also allow some informality and happy, unforeseen juxtapositions: a rigid and over-formal display, such as a line of pots with no variation, is usually off-putting.

Think of grouping your plants together like a mini border. As well as choosing taller plants, climbers and hanging subjects to give your displays height, the ideal format uses an array of staging, with some higher-level benching at the top and then plants arranged in a number of levels descending from this point, almost like a staircase. If possible, you should have several tall-growing 'accent' plants, which will give a strong vertical line, interspersed with squatter,

ABOVE **A design which begins inside and flows out into the garden**

BELOW **An embellishment of the above, with a view from a planted windowsill down to the conservatory and beyond**

ABOVE **A clever colour combination involving a bronze terracotta pot, white dolomite and trailing *Sedum morganianum***

lower-growing plants, plus species which will cascade down and help to soften the formal geometrical lines of the benches.

For displaying your plants, one of the most elegant solutions is to use Chelsea plant stands, also known as *étagères des fleurs*, which are ready-constructed series of shelves designed to fit along walls. You can also buy corner stands to continue the display right round the walls. For 'elegant', however, you can also read 'expensive'.

Trellis and other supports can look very attractive, and you have the option of allowing plants to clamber up from base level or of attaching containers to the trellis in any position from the top downwards for a trailing effect.

Trellis comes in a variety of shapes, with plain or swagged tops, and you can either retain the natural colour or choose from the fantastic palette of wood stains and finishes now on the market.

The widely available free-standing obelisks, made from wrought iron or woven cane and withes, can be used inside as well as outside in the garden. There are all sorts of wire frames, too. Look at topiary shapes, such as cones, hoops and balls that can be completely covered with unusual clambering succulents.

TYPES OF INDOOR CONTAINER

Hanging pots and baskets, wall-mounted containers filled with trailing other succulents or some of the unusual hanging cacti, such as aporocacti, or rats' tails, make wonderful

LEFT The translucence of the large planter allows the eye to focus on this magnificent trailing *Sedum sieboldii*

BELOW The unusual jar in the corner has found its proper role as a container for *Sedum morganianum*

space-filling conversation pieces. They are so easy to look after that you can have masses of them without worrying about keeping them watered daily, as you must with traditional water-guzzling baskets. You can also have an abundance of pots fastened to walls, where succulent plants will spread so happily that this is where the drought resistance of these plants can be fully appreciated. As well as traditional baskets, there are decorative metal or cane bird cages which are far kinder to plants than they are to anything with feathers, plus futuristic spiral designer baskets in galvanized steel.

You can add all kinds of interesting containers that can be moved around to vary the planting. They might, for instance, be taken out of the house to enhance your plant displays in the garden before returning to the conservatory for a period of recuperation, if necessary, or just to ring the changes. You also have the option of creating internal beds, raised up or at ground level, into which you can plant massed displays.

In your house and conservatory containers have no need to be frost-resistant, which happily means that you have fewer constraints on choice. Garden centres stock a huge range of containers which are of surprisingly good value, but junk shops and car boot sales are also good sources of interesting oddities that go well with these plants – a small flowering cactus in a porcelain cup and saucer, for instance, or a trailing plant issuing from the neck of an olive jar.

Baskets can look very pretty. Staple a good lining of black polythene to the inside, or, if the weave isn't too open, apply two or three good coats of varnish or paint (enamel or gloss), and this will also do the trick. Don't forget to pierce some drainage holes through the polythene lining.

Strawberry pots are quite difficult to maintain when they are used for their intended purpose or to grow herbs, because they can be hard to keep sufficiently wet. They make good succulent containers, however, because these plants are so much more tolerant of drought. They look

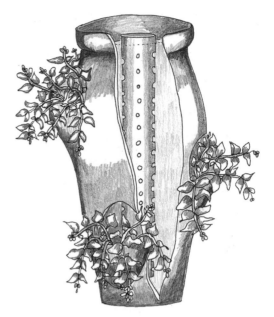

ABOVE **A strawberry pot adapted for trailing succulents**

especially attractive when planted up with trailing succulents or, for a complete change, with upright opuntias. However, even when you do use succulent plants, it can be hard to give the compost a really good soaking, especially

ABOVE **There are lots of interesting materials available to dress the surface of the container**

HOW TO MAKE A CASCADE POT

A cascade pot makes another attractive container, which can be planted up with trailing succulents. This is where pots of the same appearance but different dimensions are stacked one on top of the other, wired together and planted up with trailing succulents around the rim with a centrepiece plant in the topmost pot. For example, a stack of three, round, glazed pottery containers in a rich cobalt blue can look stunning planted with grey-leaved or green-and-gold variegated succulent plants.

There are two methods of fastening the pots together – which is necessary, because there is a lot of weight, especially in pottery structures, and you don't want your work of art to become dislodged, or to topple over and break.

In the first method, measure a length of stiff wire, long enough to pass through each pot in turn with plenty to spare. Anchor the wire in by bending it into an 'L' shape at the bottom and push it up through the drainage hole of the first pot. Fill the pot with a mixture of drainage material and compost, position the next pot above it and

ABOVE AND BELOW **Two types of self-made cascade pot**

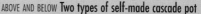

push the wire up through the drainage hole of the second pot. Centre it on top of the first and add compost. Repeat until you reach the topmost pot, pull the wire tight and bend it to secure the pots together before adding compost to the final pot and planting up.

The second method is much easier. Cut a length of bamboo cane, and position it above the central drainage hole of the first pot and anchor it in place with stones or pebbles. Fill with compost, and then centre the second pot over the first by lowering it over the cane. Carry on until you have your tower, with everything fastened together by this central rod. After filling the final pot with compost, cut the excess cane away and plant up as desired.

ABOVE *Crassula* 'Silver Springtime' makes a pretty winter display of flowers, set off by its blue ceramic pot and white top dressing

when you first plant up the pot. The narrow neck can result in water running down the outside rather than the inside of the pot. Solve this problem by inserting a length of sink pipe, cut to length and drilled with a series of regular perforations down the centre of the container. The top of the pipe should be higher than the surface of the compost to stop anything from clogging up the pipe, although you can hide it with gravel. The bottom should finish 2–3in (5–7.5cm) above the bottom of the pot. If you water down into this pipe, the water will percolate evenly through the container and into each of the side pockets.

ENSURING GOOD DRAINAGE

Ideally you should provide drainage holes in all of your containers because they can so easily and unexpectedly become waterlogged. If this is not possible, if you don't want to risk a fragile piece of china or if you are scared

ABOVE This lush display combines low-growing spreaders, a central 'statement' and cascading trailing plants in baskets

of damaging surfaces, then use a very gritty compost mix, and either mist the container occasionally or leave it rather longer than usual between waterings than you would otherwise.

Drainage holes can be added quite easily with an electric drill, but do wear goggles when you are doing this. You'll find that most containers can be drilled quite easily with a masonry drill on a slow speed; a cushion of foam or Plasticine beneath the object you are drilling can help prevent fracture, as it will dampen the sudden shock of the drill breaking through.

CHOOSING PLANTS FOR CONTAINERS

Trailing plants look well in both strawberry and cascade pots, where they can tumble out of the perforations or meander over the pot edges. You can try either a mixed planting or a single mass display of a novelty plant such as donkeys' tails (*Sedum morganianum*) or the string of beads (*Senecio rowleyanus*).

Larger hanging plants can also be combined into very low-maintenance hanging baskets. Flowering plants like epiphyllums (orchid cacti) and aporophyllums (rats' tails) make attractive drought-resistant basket choices with amazing flower displays, and these can be placed into the background when flowering is over. Cloudy masses of foliage like rhipsalis are also effective, along with the more shade-tolerant kalanchoes

ABOVE **These contrasting succulents are planted among interesting stones and 'found' objects**

and hoyas. (A quick tip: if you are planning to use hanging plants indoors, be sparing with watering and use a container with a built-in saucer to catch any drips; the safest method to protect your décor is to take the plant outside to water it.)

Tall accent plants, like aeoniums and agaves, look particularly well rising out of a carpet of scrambling and trailing succulents, which always have an attractive softening effect. And because the colour range of these plants is unusual, with pinks, purples, greys, maroon, bronze and turquoise, you have the scope to create some really unusual and exciting colour combinations.

Large bowls and other containers will look fabulous filled with a mass planting of tiny, globular-flowering cacti, such as rebutias, mammillarias and lobivias. They can create a spectacular display in the spring and early summer, and are a novel alternative to pots of spring-flowering bulbs.

Lithops or living stones are another unusual choice, especially when planted among a camouflage of rounded pebbles, from which (until they produce their white and yellow daisy heads of flowers in the autumn) they can hardly be told apart. Children love these speckled choices. They often also enjoy the challenge of

LEFT *Senecio rowleyanus* **is ideal for hanging pots and baskets**

creating a miniature garden in a bowl, using the tiny succulent plants for 'grass', 'flowers' and 'trees', perhaps with a sliver of mirror and a balsa wood bridge leading to a pebble path. Cacti are perhaps too prickly for tiny fingers.

DRESSING AND DISPLAYING CONTAINERS

You can get an interesting range of materials for top dressing your containers. Look at blue slate, which goes from pale grey when dry to glossy blue-black when wet. Dolomite is stark and white and goes well with white cobbles. Black and white chippings can look very dramatic, while the natural tones of mixed gravels and shingles give a lovely warm honey glow to pots.

ABOVE **Cristate cacti with their wavy 'brain-like' forms are interesting container plants**

CULTIVATION ADVICE FOR CONTAINERS

Cacti and succulents are unusual in that their main requirement is to dry out between waterings, and they dislike standing for long periods with 'wet feet' – especially when the weather is cool and dull. To protect them from overwatering, make sure that all your containers have a good layer of drainage material, which should be up to one-third of a large pot.

Compost requirements are flexible: you can use any houseplant compost, such as a peatfree multipurpose soilless compost, or John Innes soil-based compost (numbers 2 or 3 are fine), with the addition of horticultural grit for extra drainage to give a safety margin if you tend to be heavy-handed with watering. (A pedestal pot or a lightweight plastic pot is better with a soil-based compost, to prevent the container toppling when the compost is dry.)

The plants are tolerant, but will appreciate a good soaking approximately once a week in the growing season and feeding roughly once a month.

Between late autumn and early spring your plants should be kept dry and frost free. This dry period is essential for cacti if they are to set flower successfully the following year.

During the winter months, the 'other succulents' will need an occasional light misting in a warmer conservatory to keep them plump and hydrated, while the cacti will also need the bare minimum of water in order to prevent them from shrivelling.

You will find that many plants will survive in an unheated conservatory, but it then becomes of paramount importance to keep them as dry as possible, because the combination of wet and cold is lethal to these drought-resistant choices.

Keeping a specialist collection

Acquiring and managing a specialist collection is a fascinating hobby, which can lead into anything from competing on the show bench to visiting plant habitats in the Arizona desert or the South African Cape.

A small greenhouse or conservatory can house a comprehensive collection and there are many ways to organize your plants.

ABOVE **These caudiciforms are grouped by the way they have adapted to drought by producing almost sculptural storage organs**

You may choose to put together a representative collection covering the whole spread of succulent plants, including cacti and other succulents from all over the world. In this case, collectors often like to display their plants grouped according to their geographical origins.

Other collectors enjoy assembling a specialist collection covering a specific genus, such as the mammillarias, for example, which are interesting for their shape, spines and flowers. Other approaches include a collection based on a type of adaptation – such as the caudiciforms – or centred around a single area, such as the South African succulents or the cacti of Mexico.

Whatever you choose, display here takes second place to the organizational side and to record-keeping. Even so, your collection will look best if you use a uniform style and colour of pot, in a range of sizes. Label every plant clearly, indelibly and accurately with its correct name. You may also want to record where and when you obtained an individual plant, and other information, such as field collection data. If you want to keep a lot of data, a log book or computer database can store all the information you want to record.

Many succulent plants are endangered in habitat, so only buy plants from legitimate sources that comply with CITES (the Convention on International Trade in Endangered Species of Wild Fauna and Flora, www.cites.org), which is an international agreement between governments that aims to ensure that international trade in specimens of wild animals and plants does not threaten their survival. Never be tempted to buy material that has been collected unscrupulously. The British Cactus and Succulent Society (www.bcss.org.uk) with informative magazines and a thriving network of

local branches, will put you in touch with other collectors and provide all the information that you need for developing your collection and showing your plants.

ABOVE This fabulous display of immaculately labelled cacti in peak condition was staged by Southfield Nursery in Bourne, Lincolnshire, eastern England at the Chelsea Show, London, southern England

ABOVE Some people love these plants too much to specialize and enjoy creating and caring for a mixed display like this one

ABOVE There is scope for a more artistic display, like these cacti bedded into sand and rocks and set against a painted backdrop

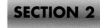

SECTION 2

CHAPTER 3

Planning an outdoor scheme

Although there is always the temptation to get started straight away on the ground, this can be wasteful – not only in the monetary sense but also in terms of time, patience and sheer hard work. Your scheme should therefore be planned as carefully as possible beforehand.

WHAT IS THE SCALE OF SCHEME YOU ARE PLANNING?

First decide whether you are looking at the design and implementation of an individual feature or a full-scale makeover of your whole garden or backyard. Whatever the scale of the scheme, it is advisable to plot your site carefully. If you are designing an individual feature, you need to look at the site as a whole to see how it will fit in with existing features. A full-scale re-design should still be broken down into a number of areas and features, which can be planned individually, with integration into a whole borne in mind.

Although it is anathema to many people, it will pay dividends to measure up and plot your garden onto graph paper, as it is suprisingly hard to sketch out the proportions accurately from memory or by guesswork. This plotting will take two of you unless you are particularly adept with a tape measure. If your site is regular, it is quite easy to pace out, or preferably to measure the dimensions, and transfer them to scale onto your graph paper.

In the case of irregular features, you can use triangulation to get the dimensions down on paper. Please don't stop reading here! I saw maths as 'time out' for daydreaming when I was at school and even I think that it really couldn't be easier.

Step 1 is to find two fixed features that are permanent, say two trees, one washing line post to the other, a shed wall to a fence, or whatever. Measure the distance between these two points, A to B, and transfer this line A–B as a scale measurement onto your plan.

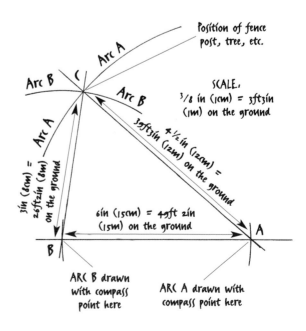

Position of fence post, tree, etc.

SCALE:
³/8 in (1cm) = 3ft3in (1m) on the ground

ABOVE **Make a scale drawing of your garden feature to help you visualize your scheme.**
Then sketch in the plants and hard landscaping you would like to use

Step 2 is to measure the distance from A and then from B to the feature C which you want to locate accurately on your plan. This gives you figures for the length of A–C and B–C. Change these measurements to your scale measurements for the plan.

Step 3. Take a pair of compasses and fix them at the scale measurement of A–C, put the point in at A and draw an arc. Repeat for B–C. C is located where the two arcs intersect on your plan.

By transferring these measurements to your plan and joining them up you will get the accurate scale dimensions of your site. If you

have lots of awkward curves and angles, repeat the triangulation exercise as often as you need until you have the shape transferred to your drawing. Once you have your shape marked out, go to an upstairs window (if you have one) or to another high vantage point and check to make sure it looks correct. (This is a bit like checking your calculator totals roughly in your head, just to make sure that you haven't entered something incorrectly.) If you really have a maths phobia, can't face the planning and measuring stage, and you are determined to get going, then take a few minutes longer to observe your

ABOVE **This is the hardy scheme illustrated on page 33 with mixed succulent yuccas, carpeting sedums, sempervivums and complementary architectural specimens like phormiums, *Cordyline australis* and *Trachycarpus fortunei*. It made dramatic growth over a period of three years**

garden from your vantage point, as it is surprisingly difficult not to lose sight of the overall shape and scale of your garden when you are looking at in on the ground.

After you have measured out your site and transferred the measurements, mark out all the major fixed features, such as hard landscaping, paths, walls, steps and patios, plus any larger features that you are planning to keep, such as vegetable plots, borders and mature trees. If you have access to a photocopier, or can reach a copy shop, make several copies that you can then draw onto until you get the scheme you like the best. Alternatively, invest in a big pad of tracing paper so that, again, you can try several versions. Whatever you do, it is advisable to keep a basic copy of the plan, because you are almost guaranteed to use it again. However sure you are that your final design really is final, you may be surprised to find the inspiration that can strike you when you are actually out in the garden constructing your scheme. Don't be afraid to modify your plans if inspiration suddenly strikes, or something just doesn't look right; most people make some changes even if they have paid a professional designer.

It is also incredibly useful to take a set of photographs of the site. You can draw your new features onto the pictures with a marker pen so that you can get a three-dimensional impression of how your garden or feature is going to look. Of course, if you are good at drawing you can bypass this step and sketch your dream landscape instead. And don't forget that there are also a large number of garden design programs for your computer, although you will still need to get out there with your tape measure and notebook to obtain the correct dimensions in the first place.

If you are lucky enough to have the budget for a garden designer and/or a landscaping contractor, I suggest you use the guidelines you would for choosing a builder and try to find a personally recommended professional whose work you can take a look at. And make sure that you get on! Some people want someone else to come up with the creative ideas; other people have an idea of exactly what they want with no room for manoeuvre. So do make absolutely certain that whoever you choose understands precisely what you require from them. It's your garden and it should express and realize your dreams – unless they are totally impractical of course, in which case the designer should be able to show you how a version of your fantasy can be brought into existence.

WHAT IS THE ASPECT OF YOUR SITE?

Your garden plan should give you the basics of the size and shape of your garden, but other features are also very important and will strongly affect the type of scheme you can have. First of all, add the direction your garden faces to your plan, as these plants will require the maximum amount of light and sun, so you need to plan for south or southwest-facing features if possible. Reserve your northerly aspects for your shade-loving plants and mini-woodland corners!

Again, you will want a well-drained position, unless you are considering a rockery or raised bed, which will automatically give you a garden with drier conditions. Consider how exposed the site is, because a sheltered site provides a much more favourable microclimate for your plants. Look at how much windproofing you have already and what you might need to add. It is often overlooked factors, such as wind damage and a high water table, that take their toll on more tender plants rather than cold as such, so an enormous amount can be done to make their conditions of growth more favourable. For example, lewisias and agaves can both be borderline for hardiness, but will be infinitely more resilient if they are planted in free-draining soil at a 45-degree angle, so that water drains out of the rosettes of leaves. Think of the cliffs in the Spanish Costa Brava resorts like Lloret and Blanes. All those postcards of agaves, silhouetted against the scarlet and gold sunset skies, show them growing at an acute angle, with enormous flower spikes towering above them. Since *Agave americana* is sometimes known as the century plant for its renowned tardiness to flower, the postcard specimens are obviously telling you something about the conditions that they like.

TYPICAL PLANT HARDINESS ZONES FOR WESTERN EUROPE

WHERE DO YOU LIVE?

Before splashing out on plant purchases for permanent planting, take a good look at your geographical location, both in a broad sense and in the local sense, where factors like a town or open countryside location make a great difference because of the effects of local microclimates that exist in towns and cities. Raw temperatures are important, of course, and factors including how many hours of cold weather there are in winter, how hot the summers are and whether the climate is damp or dry, but look too at your height above sea level and your rainfall levels. Then there are also purely local features, such as being sited in a localized frost pocket, to consider.

HARDINESS ZONES

For many years the Americans have used the Harvard University-derived system of 'hardiness

TYPICAL PLANT HARDINESS
ZONES FOR NORTH AMERICA

Keys to colours (both maps)

⬤	Zone 1:	below −50°F (−46°C)
⬤	Zone 2:	−50 to −40°F (−46 to −40°C)
⬤	Zone 3:	−40 to −30°F (−40 to −34.5°C)
⬤	Zone 4	−30 to −20°F (−34 to −29°C)
⬤	Zone 5	−20 to −10°F (−29 to −23°C)
⬤	Zone 6	−10 to 0°F (−23 to −18°C)
⬤	Zone 7	0 to 10°F (−18 to −12°C)
⬤	Zone 8	10 to 20°F (−12 to −7°C)
⬤	Zone 9	20 to 30°F (−7 to −1°C)
⬤	Zone 10	30 to 40°F (−1 to 4°C)
⬤	Zone 11	above 40°F (above 4°C)

zones' to judge how plants will grow and which species will thrive. This can also be adapted for use in Europe and the UK. Cacti have evolved in the southern states of the USA and in South America, so they are the obvious choice for your garden in these zones, and they are an excellent solution to the problems

37

ABOVE **Hardy cacti and succulents look very effective against gravel, cobbles and paving in this unusual border, thriving in a sunny south-facing front garden in the East Midlands, England**

of gardening in hot and dry areas where water is at a premium. This is also true of the Mediterranean climate zones, including the Mediterranean basin in Europe, South Africa (where indigenous cactus-like plants have evolved as a result of parallel evolution), and Western Australia (although there are restrictions on the plants that can be grown in Australia in case of unwanted naturalization).

Below these Zone 9 regions, many cacti and other succulents can be grown with little difficulty in Zone 8, so long as you avoid the species that cannot tolerate any frost. Luckily there are lots of tough species to choose from (see the plant directory, pages 104–149, for ideas), some of which will thrive down to Zone 6, and there are species of cacti that are reportedly winter hardy to Zone 3 in Canada (which can tolerate winter temperatures to about −30°F (−34°C), including *Opuntia compressa* and *Opuntia fragilis*.

The secret here lies in considering the plants' evolutionary development. In general, they can tolerate a lot of cold as long as they are *dry*, but they hate to be cold and wet, so avoid low-lying or exposed areas. Establish your plants as early as possible in the season so they have a long time to develop a root system. Take advantage of the microclimates in your garden or yard, by planting in the shelter of a south-facing or southwest-facing wall, which blocks the wind and acts like a storage heater by holding the sun's heat and by 'borrowing' escaped heat from the house.

Many areas within the USA and much of mainland Europe have a so-called 'continental climate', where large land masses and great distances from the sea mean that there are temperature extremes, as the land mass warms up and cools down dramatically and the climate is relatively dry. These areas are basically mild or warm and often dry, with hot summers and often extremely cold winters. However, cacti and other succulents will survive short periods of very low temperatures if the average winter temperature is not too bad and if they are grown in a well-drained position. Of course, the hardiness zones refer to minimum temperatures but not to how long the cold spells last, so a climate zone with prolonged cold during the day or night creates more restrictions on you. However, there are techniques to protect the plants in really cold areas. Rule one is that if you cannot bear to lose the plant, either keep it inside for the winter or ensure you have plenty of cuttings as a back-up if disaster strikes.

If you are really worried, then you can use horticultural fleece or bubble wrap, paper or cloth as a temporary blanket to cover the plants during cold spells – remove any impermeable material, such as polythene or bubble wrap, in the morning, as it will create condensation underneath as the plant warms up. You can also construct a mini glasshouse or cold frame from clear plastic or glass sheets for winter protection or, with the advice of a qualified electrician, consider running heating wires through the beds.

However harsh your climate, you will find that *all* cacti and other succulents can be bedded out for the summer months and will really enjoy the natural light and a freer root run. In really cold areas, plants can be wrapped up or moved in to a conservatory or greenhouse for the winter and back out to create an exciting summer bedding scheme the following season.

Milder, but rainier areas, have the damp 'maritime climate' of seaboard regions, like much of the UK and other areas where the ocean prevents the land from cooling down or heating beyond certain limits. It is often wet conditions rather than the cold that damages or destroys plants so, in this situation, planting in an elevated position with sloping beds, sharp drainage and perhaps some overhead protection will all help you to keep your garden looking good. Try adding sand to the soil, as it will warm up faster after a cold spell than a heavier soil (although this does not work in areas with prolonged cold such as northern Europe and the central and eastern coast of the USA).

ABOVE **This interesting mixed planting, which can be seen at Exeter University in the southwest of England, uses a hardy opuntia as a dramatic focal point**

In areas with wet winters, such as the USA Pacific north-west and northern Europe, you can think about creating a waterproof canopy in the winter or perhaps planting under a covered pergola, and again use raised, sloping, sharply drained beds. You may have an area with an overhanging balcony, say, which will help keep plants drier, though the benefits of this protection are cancelled out if the plot is too shady as a result. Protect the 'collar' of the plant, where the stem and root system meet, by keeping it clear of the soil and pouring a good layer of fine gravel around it so that it drains quickly.

HOW MUCH EFFORT ARE YOU PREPARED TO PUT INTO MODIFYING YOUR SITE?

You can do a lot to modify your particular site to make it more favourable to plants and therefore to expand the range of plants you can use in your scheme.

Windproofing the area to create a sheltered planting feature will automatically raise the temperature and also protect your plants from damage. If you are planning one feature, look

ABOVE Although many cacti and succulents are need winter protection, they all enjoy being outside in dramatic summer bedding schemes

for a ready-made sheltered position, such as house walls, the right angle where the garage wall perhaps projects forward from the house, an enclosed patio, and so on. You may have existing hedges and fencing; if not, are you prepared to spend time and money on adding these? There are all sorts of possibilities offered by trellis panels and other ornamental structures, which both divide spaces and act as protection, and also help to divide up garden features,

particularly very dissimilar ones, such as an ornamental garden from a vegetable garden, or a wild garden from a formal garden. This gives a series of 'garden rooms', where the garden is revealed little by little as you move around in it, which can add interest and apparent size. Make sure the resulting space is not too gloomy for the plants, however.

If you have a wall at the back of your feature, this has the advantage of acting like a storage heater, absorbing the heat of the sun and releasing it over a period of time, which gives your plants more favourable conditions. You can also consider painting the wall a lighter colour to reflect and maximize the warmth of the sun.

If you have a high water table or your plants have to be at the bottom of a slope, you have the choice of constructing an unusual rockery, or a raised bed to improve drainage. If you don't want a rise in the level, you can also improve the soil by digging in quantities of gravel, laying land drains, or draining the area into a pond.

As mentioned above, it's also important to select the most favourable aspect, i.e. south or southwest-facing if possible. In extreme cases you may have to rotate your garden so that your exotic feature is at the furthermost end of your site. For example, you may have to site a feature like a patio or a summer house against a far wall or fence if proximity to the house means that you would have to set your plants in a cold and shady position.

WHAT SAFETY FACTORS NEED TO BE TAKEN INTO ACCOUNT?

When your plan includes spiky plants, water features, rockeries, raised terraces, steep steps or decking, you have to consider who will be using your garden. Although these features can look fabulous, they are not necessarily the safest or most user-friendly options. You may have to reconsider if you have young children and/or inquisitive pets. There are also constraints when designing for the elderly, or for those with disabilities, if, for example, you need to make provision for wheelchair access, or handrails on steps and other features.

If you have children or pets, spikes may need to be trimmed off some of the agaves and yuccas, for example, or the plants need to be situated well away from exploratory fingers or noses. Children can drown in quite literally a few inches or centimetres of water, so a pond may need to be put on hold. If you have to have the sight and sound of water, there are safe and attractive alternatives where the water is contained in an underground tank and bubbles up safely through a millstone or out of a water feature onto stones.

Low-maintenance, drought-resistant cacti and other succulents are ideal in many ways for the elderly or disabled. Raised beds can offer a combination of advantages, affording ease of access and maintenance for the gardener along with a well-drained position for the plants.

HOW MUCH TIME DO YOU WANT TO SPEND?

This is a key question you need to ask yourself. In many ways this sort of gardening is far less demanding than the more traditional garden, with its annual bedding, its herbaceous borders and its lawn to care for.

A mixed scheme will generally require the most attention during the spring and autumn months, when half-hardy material is planted out and lifted, and will require some forethought and planning for over-wintering the more tender plants.

However, there is alternative option which is halfway between two: you could have a fully hardy permanent planting, with the addition of moveable containers that are planted with half-hardy subjects. These will just need moving in and out of the house in synchronization with the seasons. Containers will also provide you with the added benefit of a burst of colour and interest indoors during the winter.

ABOVE Succulents, like fully hardy *Sedum cauticola* 'Lidakense' and *S. pachyclados*, growing here by the pond-side, make colourful, low-maintenance choices

AND HOW MUCH MONEY CAN YOU SPEND?

Most gardens mature over time. This, therefore, is another case for taking a good look at your plan of the garden, and experimenting by drawing in various combinations of the plants that will make the strongest architectural statement over time, before you actually purchase anything.

41

CHAPTER 4

Gravel and scree beds

ABOVE **This gravel garden is full of unusual colours and texture, making an easy-to-care-for and very different patio surround**

Gravel and scree gardens are very flexible because they have so many applications. They can be used for a single border, an island bed, a front garden, or the awkward weedy strip along the edge of a driveway.

The smaller gardens and yards of newer houses are particularly suitable for these schemes because they create such a visual impact and make a more dramatic statement than anything else you may consider. Trying to fit a traditional garden into the space can be really frustrating. Gravel and scree gardens make much more sense in a smaller space than trying to fit in a tiny lawn and surrounding it with a high-maintenance border, with the nightmare task of keeping the grass regularly mown, weed free and neatly edged.

WHAT ARE GRAVEL AND SCREE BEDS?

In a gravel bed, the whole surface of a bed, border or other feature is covered with a mulch comprising an assortment of materials which can range from a layer of fine gravel, such as pea shingle, to coloured chippings or bark. For the more adventurous there are various other materials to choose from, ranging from shells to industrial waste glass which has been transformed into a smooth covering material in the form of coloured fine glass pebbles without any sharp edges.

Scree gardens differ in that the gravel surface is used in combination with carefully selected pieces of larger material. This larger material consists of either rounded or jagged rock forms in diminishing sizes. For example, from large, water-smoothed boulders, through cobbles to small, rounded pebbles or larger pieces of rock diminishing gradually in size until there is a rough scree of broken rock pieces blending into the gravel. The conceit here is that there is a reference to the natural scree features, which form at the bottom of steep cliff faces, where the rocks lie in a jumble. In scree gardening the scree area can link a gravel bed to a rockery, or the larger rocks and stones can act as extra features, chosen and 'planted' almost in the same way that the living specimens are, and used to bind the scheme together as a whole.

SITING

These beds have to have a definite demarcation between the gravel and the next material, be it grass, garden soil or hard landscaping. You don't want gravel or other top dressing straying into lawns, or grass growing into the gravel. If your lawn has too big a hold on your affections and has therefore been reprieved, add a strip of paving or other edging to run between the edge of the gravel bed and the edge of the lawn. If its profile is lower than the lawn, you can mow straight over the edges, which maintains a tidy boundary between your different garden areas.

If you would like to grow the widest range of plants, the bed should be south- or southwest-facing and a wall at the back of the site will increase the range of plants you can use, because it will give shelter and act as a 'storage heater'. You should also consider windproofing the bed with larger plants, or fencing or trellis.

CONSTRUCTION

For low maintenance, you must use a permeable membrane, which lets moisture through to the roots but suppresses weeds. I really cannot stress

ABOVE **If you have a large area to cover, cut down the undergrowth and roll out the membrane to smother the weeds. Anchor each strip with bricks or stones until you put the gravel on**

this point too strongly, because it is easy to use, relatively cheap and will save literally hours and hours of work in the long run. Contrary to popular belief, gravel doesn't kill weeds, so don't believe any one who tells you that gravel is a perfect, weed-suppressing mulch. After all, people are advised to plant seeds and cuttings in a sharp mixture of gritty compost – in effect in a gravel bed! Unlined gravel over soil is a perfect seedbed for every plant and weed within bird, wind or pet transmission.

Black polythene is a short-term solution, but it will eventually become brittle and then crack in daylight, especially where the gravel has moved and exposed it. It will also collect standing water. However, permeable membrane is ultra-violet stabilized, so that it will not become brittle and perish. It is water permeable, so that puddles do not form on the surface, and it has a dense black finish, which suppresses the growth of weeds and also prevents the roots of your

ABOVE Vivid blue *Kleinia repens* makes a brilliant splash in this two-level gravel bed filled with succulent plants

cultivated plants from surfacing. It is also air permeable, so that the soil does not become sour or acidified. The membrane comes on a roll; you can choose from a variety of widths from 20in (0.5m) to 16ft (5m) wide, although a 3ft (1m) width is probably the easiest to manage. It is usually printed with 'tramlines', so that it is easy to line up one sheet with another, and to plant in straight lines if necessary.

Clear the site, removing as many weeds as possible. You can consider a scorched earth policy with herbicides such as Tumbleweed or Roundup, which will take about three weeks to kill weeds in all but will give you a clean site. If you are replacing a lawn, skim off the turf for use elsewhere, or stack it upside-down in a corner of your garden where it will rot down into an excellent garden compost. You can actually cover whatever is already there, e.g. a lawn,

weeds, etc., because the weight of the material and the darkness of the membrane will smother and kill anything underneath it. (Think of the appearance of the grass on a campsite when a ground sheet has been taken away!)

Unroll the membrane and cut the first strip to length, ensuring that it is parallel to any relevant straight edge, such as the edge of a path or patio, house wall, etc. The first strip should be butted well up to the edge of the site. If you are lucky enough you can put the edges under paving that already exists, otherwise consider edging with bricks or slabs, because you don't want the soil underneath the membrane to trickle over the edges onto the top surface, where it will contaminate your covering material.

You can buy special accessories for anchoring the membrane down. These range from a simple prong-like staple (like a capital E without the central bar), which come in two sizes, either 4 x 6in (10 x 15cm) or 4 x 9in (10 x 23cm) to a range of toothed spikes that are about 6in (15cm) long (which look like Christmas trees standing on their heads), and an adhesive tape for joining the lengths together. None of these are absolutely vital, because a few old bricks or big stones will also do the trick by holding the liner down, and once the gravel is down the weight will hold the membrane firmly in place. However, you will definitely need to use them if you are covering a sloping site.

If you have a completely clear site, you can cover the whole area with horizontal strips, allowing about a 6in (15cm) overlap. If you are keeping any plants, you will have to work around these, almost as you would do when wallpapering around light switches. You will need to slit the membrane as you lay it, and then tuck the cut ends neatly around the base of the resident plants. Once you have a smooth, membrane-covered site, your gravel bed will be ready for planting up.

CHOOSING YOUR PLANTS
SELECTIONS THAT CAN SURVIVE THE WINTER

Larger plants include the hardy agave and other spiky plants, such as the yucca, plus tall cacti like hardy opuntias. *Crassula sarcocaulis* makes an attractive miniature tree, with a slender trunk and a spreading canopy of small dark green leaves. In the summer it bears a mass of tiny pink flowers which virtually cover the plant. *Puya chilensis* is a short, woody-stemmed shrub which is crowned by a dense rosette of long, tapering, arching leaves, and bearing remarkable, tubular metallic-yellow flowers. However, it is ferociously spined, so it's definitely not a good choice for the child- or pet-friendly garden. I suggest you look, too, at *Agave palmeri* var. *chrysantha* and *A. parryi* and, in milder areas and in the city microclimates, at *A. americana*.

There is also a good range of lower-growing subjects. Smaller globular cacti, such as lobivias, chamaecereus and echinopsis, combine well with sempervivums, or house leeks, which come in a wonderful colour spectrum from cobwebbed white and green through to purple and caramel. A mixture of sedums, including the striking green and maroon *S. rubrum* and purple-coloured *S. spathulifolium* var. *purpureum*, set alongside frosty purple-grey *S. spathufolium* 'Cape Blanco' makes an eye-catching display. Look, too, at encrusted saxifrages, lewisias, and the grey-green mats of *Delosperma cooperi*, which bears lilac flowers from spring until the first frost and the pale green sheet of *Delosperma nubigenum* with its mass of yellow daisy-like flowers in the spring.

HALF-HARDY SELECTIONS

Tall columnar cereus plus cactus-like euphorbias, such as *Euphorbia cooperi*, which will grow a 3ft (1m) high cactus-like candelabra, will furnish your beds. Many aeoniums are wonderfully structural plants, with naked grey trunks with a multitude of branches, growing in an unusual candelabra-like form. These stems can grow to

ABOVE **This scree bed, which has a soil composition of mainly scree and gravel, supports a contented colony of hardy *Opuntia compressa***

LEFT Aloes, sempervivums, cacti and delosperma are interwoven with *Agave americana* and flowering gazanias in this tiered gravel bed

ASSOCIATED ARCHITECTURAL PLANT CHOICES

Some of the many plants which associate very sympathetically with cacti and other succulents include ornamental grasses such as the blue-leaved *Festuca glauca* and *F.* 'Golden Toupee' and the grass-like, black-leaved *Ophiopogon planiscapus* 'Nigrescens'. Larger choices for containers include variegated forms such as gardener's garters (*Phalaris arundinacea* var. *picta*), or *Cortaderia selloana* (pampas grass), the well-known hardy evergreen, with arching foliage and wonderful silvery flower plumes, which makes a lovely specimen plant and is seen at its best in splendid isolation.

Try the hardiest palms such as *Chamaerops humilis* and *Trachycarpus fortunei*, plus the lush fronds of *Dicksonia antarctica*, the hardy tree fern. For huge subjects, reaching up to 15ft (4.5m) high, look at the elegant clumps of the black bamboo, *Phyllostachys nigra*, or the golden bamboo, *P. aurea*.

BEDDING YOUR PLANTS

Before setting the plants, arrange them loosely on the surface of the membrane until you are happy with the arrangement. As a good rule of thumb, large accent plants should be set singly to make an exclamation mark in the bed; smaller plants should follow the rule of sets of three or five. If they are set in odd-numbered clumps, this will give a well-filled arrangement that does not appear too regimented. It is best to avoid even-numbered clumps because they always look very 'blocky' and unnatural.

Once you are happy with the scheme, take each plant in turn and lay it to one side of its planting position. Use a sharp knife, like a Stanley knife, a box cutter, or a good-sized pair of sharp scissors, to slit a large cross shape in

3ft (1m) high, and are topped with tightly packed, almost flower-like, rosettes of leaves. *Aeonium arboreum* has bright green rosettes which contrast superbly well with spectacular purple-black *Aeonium arboreum* 'Zwartkop'.

The money plant, *Crassula ovata*, is an attrative miniature tree, with glossy, coin-shaped, succulent leaves and a gnarled trunk. It has colourful varieties, such as the grey-green 'Blue Bird' and the variegated green, yellow and red 'Hummel's Sunset'. These three make a good 'pick and mix' combination.

the membrane, up to 3ft (1m) in each direction, depending, of course, on the size of the plant. Peel the four sections back on themselves, just as you would peel an orange, to expose the soil underneath. You then need to dig a generous hole to accommodate the root ball with plenty of room to spare. Use sacking or surplus liner to put the excavated soil onto and drop the plant into the hole, with the junction of the soil with the plant kept at the level the plant was already at in its previous site or container.

Water the plant in well, unless the ground is sodden. If your soil is particularly heavy this is a good opportunity to improve it by adding some gravel or horticultural grit to increase drainage. You can also add granular plant food at this stage. Fill in around the root ball with some of the soil you have taken out, pushing it well in and firming the plant so that none of the roots will be in air pockets. Don't overdo the firming in, though, because air needs to get to the roots. Tramp the ground down well around the neck of the plant, then fold the membrane back and tuck it around the collar of the plant.

DRESSING THE BED

When all of the plants have been set, dress the whole bed with up to 3in (7.5cm) depth of your chosen top dressing, although you can get away with as little as 1in (2.5cm) on a flat site. The quickest way to lay your top dressing is to use a wheelbarrow and tip out conical heaps from it at regular intervals along the strips of membrane. Then, using a really stiff broom, you can actually 'sweep' the dressing out across the membrane in a nice, even layer. However, this will only work with a dry surfacing material. The other method is to use a reversed spade and to pull the mulch towards you in even strokes until it has been spread out over the whole surface.

As far as your choice of top dressing goes, there is a much greater choice of interesting materials to choose from nowadays, and none will break the bank. The cheapest materials are straightforward bark chippings or cocoa shells, seashells or fine pea shingle. Along with these, there is a vast range of larger pebbles to choose from: tiny stones, through to cobbles and up to huge, rounded boulders, which can be used in attractive combinations. These options have the advantages that always come from natural-looking materials, in that the colours tend to be warm and harmonious.

Currently there is a boom in gardening, which has motivated vast numbers of previously uninterested people to take a new pride and

ABOVE **You can incorporate existing plants by cutting the membrane to shape around the base of the plant, rather as you would wallpaper around a light switch**

ABOVE **Lay the gravel in a generous layer, which will anchor the membrane and smother any weed growth**

ABOVE **After the bed is covered in gravel, you can decorate It with rocks and containers**

enthusiasm in their gardens as an extension of their household DIY projects. This means that the giant DIY multiples and superstores have now moved into the supply of hard landscaping products on a vast scale, which has reduced the price of previously expensive materials to the level of everyone's budget. Of course, there will always be a place for the unique, higher-cost, hard-to-source finishes in gardens that have a larger budget. For the everyday household, though, it is nice to be able to ring the changes with coloured slates, for example, available in red and blue-grey, which give an interesting finish with a reflective sheen. Gravels can be found in an array of colours – from black, white and grey, through two-tones like black and white, and on to more dramatic red, green and blue. The smoothed glass chippings already mentioned also come in a range of frosted colours, which are both bold and attractive.

There is a cornucopia of special effects available with these coloured materials, achieved by butting one type against another, but this is not for the faint-hearted. You may have seen raked Japanese gravel gardens and be entranced by the concept of a sort of 'texture lawn', with its connotations of peace and spiritual tranquillity. However, there is anything but tranquillity in store unless you are prepared to sink an edging material such as lawn edging, or to use rows of brick pavers, or other material, to keep the colours separate. Be warned! The gravel will mix and mingle and your clean edges will rapidly lose definition.

The other point with gravel is that it strays. So if you are going to use these gravelled areas as pathways to other parts of the garden, you should perhaps consider sinking paving stones at intervals into the through routes to act as stepping stones; otherwise, gravel will inevitably be walked onto adjoining surfaces. It is also uncomfortable for people wearing open-toed sandals or high heels.

ABOVE **The completed scheme links a pond with a living edge of succulents including** *Mesembryanthemum* **'Basutoland', irises and phormiums, and a rockery planted with agaves and echeverias**

ABOVE After a year, the gravel garden looks as if it has been there for ever. *Phormium tenax* 'Variegatum' is in bud in the foreground

ABOVE **Half-hardy echeverias really colour up in natural light. Here they glow like jewels against this bed dressed with blue slate**

HOW TO KEEP IT LOOKING GOOD

As already mentioned, this is low-maintenance gardening, so gravel and scree beds are very easy to care for, and are much less effort than traditional lawns and borders.

As long as you line the beds with membrane, there is never much weeding to be done. Some weeds can get a foothold in wetter weather, when the gravel remains wet for a longer period than usual, but you will find that they are very lightly rooted because of the membrane, so they come up very easily. The site can also be sprayed with a chemical herbicide – with care. I suggest you use a sheet of cardboard, held vertically between the weeds and the plants, to protect the plants from the spray.

Other than the weeding there is general housekeeping, like tidying up straggly plants. As cordylines, agaves and yuccas grow they make new leaves and the outer leaves die off. When the leaves are withered, pull them off with a really sharp, downward tug, and this will reveal the exotic trunks of the plants. Yuccas flower regularly each year, producing cream spikes of pendant, tulip-like flowers. Remove the dead flower spikes, as water can accumulate in the remains during winter.

You can use kitchen tongs to remove dead petals from between the leaves, if necessary. Over time, you will need to divide up spreading plants like phormiums and the smaller succulents. This gives you new plants for using elsewhere. Look out for invasive plants that may swamp their shyer neighbours if they are not treated with a firm hand. Fortunately, these invasive plants can easily be divided up, and a smaller section replanted, if required, while you will have plenty of new material for further projects.

51

CHAPTER 5

Unusual rockeries

Cacti and other succulents, along with other architectural plants, offer an interesting alternative to the traditional rockery and they lend themselves especially well to this situation. These plants are less vigorous, so the rockery stays under control more easily than when it is planted with more

ABOVE *Echinocereus viridiflorus* is happy in this sunny spot, where the rocks give it shelter from the weather

rampant, carpeting choices. The raised, free-draining position also suits the plants particularly, and cacti and other succulents can sometimes be grown in a rockery in a less than favourable geographical position when they would surely perish if they were planted directly into the level ground.

You can use cacti and other succulents for a radically different and somewhat minimalist planting scheme or succulent, carpeting plants if you prefer a busier, well-filled look. The plants will also mix effectively together with careful planting; alternatively, they can make surprising or subtle additions to your existing rockery, whether it is planted with alpines, miniature bulbs, dwarf conifers or indeed any of these in combination.

CHOOSING YOUR PLANTS

Scale is important in this type of gardening; you will mostly be using smaller-growing subjects to tuck into crevices and pockets of soil. Therefore, as a rule, you should choose taller accent plants that will grow no more than a foot or two high (30–60cm), medium-sized plants in the 6in–1ft (15–30cm) range, and tiny carpeting plants under 6in (15cm) tall (though these often have indefinite spread, so they have to be watched!).

For a really radical look, you can plant up your rockery entirely with hardy cacti. The hardy opuntias make wonderful subjects; with a variety

ABOVE **Cacti and other succulents thriving on this sandstone cliff in southern England bedded in pockets of compost mixed with cement**

of forms to stand as sentinels or scramble among your rocks. However, if you are going to use cacti in a rockery, it is a good idea to consider using a membrane, as weeding these subjects is almost impossible once they are growing vigorously because of their spines. You can also consider some of the hardier small globular cacti, such as chamaecereus and lobivia, which will make a good contrast in size and shape.

Alternatively, you can plant a mixture of lower-growing shrubby succulents with some trailing subjects for another take on the more traditional approach, or combine both cacti and other succulents. Because of the scale of the plants,

cacti and other succulents mix well with alpines, and there is a cross-over of species in that there is a whole group of succulent alpines to consider, including sedums and crassulas.

If you want to extend your range of plants, mix in some half-hardy subjects. If you tuck them into position in their pots, they can be removed to safety for the winter and returned the next spring

You can also go for a Japanese feel, with lower-growing bamboos and tiny grasses, interspersed with interesting pebbles and rocks. Bonsai-like succulents, which take the form of miniature trees, like hardy *Crassula sarcocaulis*, combine well with this type of rockery. There are

53

ABOVE **Echeverias and sempervivums scramble attractively over these old terracotta plant pots**

also the tree-like half-hardy specimens, such as *Crassula ovata*, *Aichryson dichotomum*, *Sedum frutescens* or *Portulacaria afra* 'Foliisvariegatus', with its red stems and variegated foliage, which make pretty houseplants in the winter.

ABOVE **Planting up a stratified rockery with hardy cacti in a gritty soil mixture for maximum drainage**

You can pot these up in shallow earthenware dishes, where they can function as instant 'bonsai'; they make an attractive finishing touch, lined up on a wall, or along steps, near your Japanese-style rockery, where they can stand out for the summer and move indoors as the weather gets colder. The shallow earthenware saucers meant for some of the larger pots make really cheap bonsai bowls. You will need to drill the base with a couple of holes for drainage, and plant up your little tree or trees with suitable rocks and stones.

SITING

Because cacti and other succulents like a well-drained position, rockeries offer almost ideal conditions, and in less favourable areas are perhaps the only way that these plants can safely be treated as hardy. A raised, sloping, well-drained site is ideal for these plants. Ideally a sunny, south-facing slope is the first choice, preferably with some shelter from the wind and perhaps a light background to reflect the sun. The most tender subjects can be given extra protection if they are tucked into the shelter of an overhanging rock, and they should also be planted in the steepest, most vertical position that you can possibly give them.

HOW TO KEEP IT LOOKING GOOD

Weeding is going to be the main chore you have to endure, plus keeping an eye on the growth of the plants and nipping back anything that gets too invasive. In general, a rockery demands more management because there is usually an overall design which you wish to retain, so be prepared to split, thin out and remove plants. They are always there as seed corn for your next project.

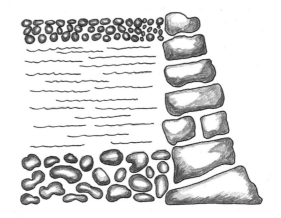

ABOVE The stones in this drystone wall, edging a raised bed, are angled backwards and downwards to make a really stable structure. Drainage material is at the bottom, under a gritty soil layer topped with gravel. You can plant into the cracks between the stones as well as into the top

BELOW This boulder rockery is planted up with an assortment of hardy cacti and other succulents, which will relish the raised soil level and free root run

CHAPTER 6

Outdoor container planting

Traditionally, container plantings have been made up of the bright summer bedding: the petunias, the busy lizzies, lobelias and nasturtium, nicotiana, and all the other sunny-faced, colourful, perpetually flowering delights. But unfortunately these traditional choices do need a good deal of care and attention in the form of watering, feeding and deadheading to keep them looking good. Nowadays, when so many of us are combining busy professional lives with our private family lives, this can be difficult. Succulents, however, have evolved a number of ways of coping with drought conditions without ill effects so they are able to withstand the punishment of hot, dry weather, and the occasional neglect that results from lives which are filled with other demands.

Apart from being both low maintenance and good looking, containers offer all sorts of other advantages, including the fact that they are immensely flexible because they are portable – you can change the whole look of your garden in moments simply by moving your containers around.

TYPES OF OUTDOOR CONTAINER

A limited budget is no longer a barrier to taste, and you don't have to settle for plastic urns and plastic 'terracotta' now unless you choose to. Terracotta pots abound, alongside all sorts of colours of low-cost glazed pots plus 'antique stone' urns, which are embellished with cherubs and armorial crests; these will bring the country house ethos into anyone's plot.

And if you do use plastic, because it's cheap, light and maybe also because it is already there, don't forget that you can customize it with aerosol paints in a multitude of attractive colours,

ABOVE *Aeonium arboreum* and *Aeonium atropurpureum* with echeverias and a phormium near a large terracotta pot make an attractive display

ABOVE This clever arrangement of pots in the garden at East Ruston Old Vicarage, Norfolk in the east of England, is reminiscent of the Victorian plant theatres

and in some wonderful metallic finishes, which include silver, gold, 'antique' copper, bronze, or matt pewter.

You can, of course, also go the whole hog and buy a wonderful, custom-made pot from a craftsman or choose one of the higher-quality imports that are available today.

RIGHT The grey foliage of *Cotyledon orbiculata* contrasts with the purple-leaved *Crassula pellucida subsp. marginalis*

ABOVE **Broken pots can make unusual containers, like this one planted with mixed succulents**

UNUSUAL CONTAINER IDEAS

Life creates an endless supply of chipped, dented, outmoded or outgrown casualties. On a small scale there are old woks and teapots, broken jugs and wicker baskets (waterproofed with a stapled black polythene lining). House bricks and perforated wall slabs can also take on entirely new identities. Old boots and shoes make surprisingly durable planters, spilling a mass of colourful sempervivums from their empty ankles and from the split and curling toe caps.

On a larger scale, you have beer barrels, stone sinks, or stone-sink look-alikes, made from glazed sinks that are treated with a peat and cement mix, as described in the panel opposite.

ABOVE **Old boots and shoes make surprisingly long-lasting and novel containers, like this pair of boots planted with mixed sempervivums**

ABOVE **This stone corner pot houses a pretty assortment of sempervivums**

CREATING A STONE SINK REPLICA

Glazed sinks can be disguised as stone sink replicas. First clean the sink and make sure that it is grease free. Coat the surface of the sink with a multipurpose adhesive, continuing the adhesive over the rim of the sink and down to below the ultimate soil level.

Mix two parts of multipurpose compost with one part of fine horticultural grit or sharp sand and one part cement. Mix with water until you have a fairly thick consistency and apply it to the tacky surfaces of the sink. You can leave the finish exactly as it is, or you can wait until it begins to harden and then you can mark the surface with indentations and irregularities for authenticity.

You can also use this mixture to construct mock stone sinks and containers. Find two cardboard boxes which will fit one inside the other with about a 3in (7.5cm) gap between them. Line the inside of the first box with cling film and cover the outside of the second one with a layer of the same material. Take the larger, empty, cling film-lined box and pour the mock stone mixture into the bottom, making up a layer of around 3in (7.5cm) deep. Stand the second box inside the first on top of the mixture and pour the remaining mixture down the gaps between the two boxes until the 'walls' reach the height you require. Wait for the mixture to set, remove your cardboard box inner and outer moulds and you have a nice 'stone' container for a fraction of the cost of the real thing. Because of the compost in the mixture, the colour and finish is very sympathetic and you will find that it quickly weathers naturally and attractively.

ABOVE **Here is another boot to stumble across, spilling bright red *Sedum album f. murale* 'Coral Carpet' from its toes, contrasting with bright yellow thyme**

There are tin baths and old wheelbarrows, right up to huge features like an old pony cart, or even an upended boat (which can also make a pretty and unusual arbour in a seaside-themed garden).

The advantages of ready portability make it very important for you to choose your materials carefully. If you intend to lug your pots around on a regular basis it is advisable to choose lighter materials, not only for the pots but also for the compost and drainage materials. However, an alternative option is to use your heavier pots as sleeves and conceal the lighter plastic pots inside them. You will then be able to swap these pots over as and when you want.

ABOVE AND RIGHT **Choose an attractive pot with drainage holes. Otherwise, drill your own holes with a masonry drill wearing protective goggles**

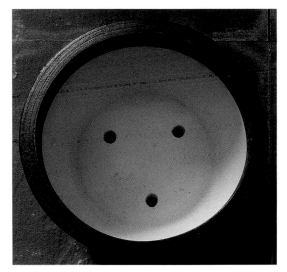

ENSURING GOOD DRAINAGE

Construction is straightforward, but containers for succulent plants do need drainage. It is only a moment's work to drill drainage holes if they aren't already there, and it is courting disaster if you don't do so. Use a masonry drill and don't forget eye protection in case fragments fly up. You can get cheap plastic goggles from DIY outlets.

As additional protection, especially if you are heavy-handed with the watering can, drainage material should be added to the bottom of the pot; this can be either broken crocks, pebbles or – an ideal lightweight solution – polystyrene packing material. This material is apparently indestructible and certainly makes for a much more portable container, although it is really tiresome to handle as it clings to clothes and swirls off around the garden on the slightest current of air. Choose a still day.

Any proprietary loam or soil-based compost like John Innes or non-soil-based multipurpose compost will do perfectly well, with the addition of a little granular feed if you are not planning to replant the container for some time. Again, it may be worth adding sharp sand or horticultural grit to make a nice, free-draining mixture.

These containers will seldom need watering, although they will appreciate a drink in the driest periods (about once a week), and will also enjoy feeding with a fertilizer formulated for tomatoes if you find the time.

SITING

Siting is not really an issue because all cacti and other succulents will be happy more or less anywhere but in dankest, sopping-wet shade. All the awkward areas in strong sunlight are perfect for containers, which are also happy in the problem dry spots, such as paving, steps, drive and path edges and around front doors. However, they will also sit happily out of sight in

ABOVE **Materials for planting up a container consisting of equal amounts of John Innes No. 3 and sharp gravel, plus crocks for drainage in the bottom, and ornamental rocks for decoration**

ABOVE Positioning a decorative rock well down in the container, so that the compost mixture holds it firmly in place

ABOVE The completed bowl, containing a mixture of cacti

shadier areas when you want to ring the changes, and you can slip them in and out of position as and when they look their best or when you fancy a new look.

You can put containers out of harm's way of children. You can also protect little fingers and pets' noses from your spikier subjects by strategic positioning when they are around. And you can avoid damage to your precious favourites during ball games, or if parties spill outside or the gathering round the barbecue gets a bit over-excited on long summer evenings.

CHOOSING YOUR PLANTS

You can use entirely low-maintenance containers or have a mixture of traditional and succulent planters for a much easier summer of plant care,

as you can look after fewer demanding plants more thoroughly. You also have the choice of selecting totally hardy plants that can stay out all the year round, with the added bonus that they are evergreen and can give some much-needed winter colour. On the other hand, you can use half-hardy plants, which will give you interesting houseplants, or fill your conservatory with shape, texture and colour in the colder months.

Almost all cacti and other succulents enjoy a spell outside in the warmer months and they will reward you with an incredible brilliance of colours; the echeverias, for example, become almost fluorescent in their pinks, lilacs and greys, and the darker subjects, such as *Aeonium arboreum* 'Zwartkop', become much blacker with natural light.

DROUGHT-RESISTANT CHOICES

Strawberry pots are wonderful planted up with a mixture of, for example, trailing sedums for an all-year-round choice, or some of the half-hardy trailing succulents such as *Crassula sarmentosa*, *C. volkensii*, *Kleinia repens*, *Senecio rowleyanus*, *Ceropegia woodii*, *Sedum morganianum*, *S. lineare* 'Variegatum', *S. stahlii* and *S. x rubrotinctum* for inside/outside containers. Hanging baskets and window boxes can also be planted up with these low-maintenance, drought-resistant hardy or half-hardy plants, and will need far less watering than the standard containers do. You can plant the cascade pots described on page 24 with a mixture of trailing subjects. For a half-hardy cascade pot, *Crassula pellucida* subsp. *marginalis* is a good choice for planting around the edge of each pot, where it will colour up into deep maroon in full light or, alternatively, it will produce larger green and red leaves in shadier conditions. *Crassula volkensii* has a similar habit. *Sedum sieboldii* f. *variegatum*, with arching blue-green leaves splashed with white variegation, is an attractive choice, or perhaps consider *Sedum lineare* f. *variegatum*, with its pale green cloud of leaves. Some of the smaller-growing echeverias can also cluster attractively around the edges of these pots. Choose a larger architectural plant in the topmost pot as a finishing touch, such as a small agave, a large echeveria, haworthia, puya or other dramatic crowning glory.

For a larger container, you could use agaves, aeonoiums, hardy opuntias, or columnar cereus surrounded by smaller globular cacti. Look, too, at the cactus-like euphorbias. *Crassula ovata* and its cultivars look good in pedestal planters.

You can also make exciting displays by combining succulent plants with more traditional bedding plants. Try, for example, standing pots containing single architectural subjects among your bedding plants in beds and borders.

ABOVE This long-established cascade pot contains half-hardy *Crassula pellucida* subsp. *marginalis*, *Echeveria elegans* and *Sedum* x *amecamecanum*, topped with *Pitcairnia ferruginea*

Alternatively, you could try a dramatic agave, for example, surrounded with summer bedding such as pansies, violas or petunias for an eye-catching and unusual display. A green and yellow striped agave such as *A. americana* 'Variegata' or *A. americana* 'Mediopicta' looks

63

ABOVE Pottery 'boots' planted with contrasting *Crassula ovata* cultivars, 'Blue Bird' and 'Hummel's Sunset'

ABOVE A whole garden of containers that will spend the winter under cover

particularly attractive with an underplanting of blue or lilac pansies or violas.

Species of echeveria and graptoveria look good either on their own in containers or in a pot surrounding a taller, more architectural plant such as a cordyline, agave or aeonium.

Smaller globular cacti, such as lobivias, chamaecereus and echinopsis, in combination with the columnar shapes of cereus and cereus species such as trichocereus and oreocereus,

can make unusual containers, especially when adorned with chunky rocks and stones. Or try a lithops (living stones) bowl; planted among stones and pebbles you can entertain children (and adults!) with a knotty 'find the plant' game.

If you don't care for the effort that is involved in moving half-hardy containers during the winter months, look at the hardy plants mentioned for use in scree beds on page 45.

HOW TO KEEP THEM LOOKING GOOD

These pots will reward you for a very long time, because they retain their good looks year on year and they need very little care.

Containers will appreciate weekly watering in the growing season, especially in hot, dry spells. If growth is your priority, many of the succulents will appreciate extra watering and feeding in the growing season; plants such as agaves, for example, will grow into strapping specimens more rapidly with more generous watering and feeding.

Hardy subjects can stay outside all the year

round and many make an attractive and colourful evergreen winter display. Remember to keep half-hardy subjects in a frost-free place; either as a display in the house or conservatory, or out of sight in a dry garage or outhouse if you prefer – although this is a pity unless you simply cannot squeeze them in anywhere.

In the growing season you will need to tidy the pots up. Pinch out straggly bits and remove dead lower leaves. Nip back trailing plants to thicken out the growth, as the cut ends will sprout several new heads. Don't forget to keep the pieces you remove. If you dry them off for a few days to ensure that the cut edges are calloused over and then push them into the pots alongside their parents, they will root very readily which, again, will result in a more generous display.

ABOVE *Aeonium atropurpureum* is a colourful and easy-care choice

ABOVE This large container has a massed planting of assorted succulents, from left to right, *Echeveria gibbiflora, Aloe arborescens, A. aristata, A. humilis, Sedum spathulifolium* var. *purpureum, Echeveria* 'Perle von Nurnberg' and *Sedum* x *rubrotinctum*

CHAPTER 7

Pools and water features

For many people a garden would not be complete without some kind of water feature, ranging from a large pond with a rockery waterfall or a fountain to a smaller feature, such as a millstone or a lion's head on a wall, with water trickling onto stones. One of the problems, however, that results from the creation of an artificial pond is finding an effective camouflage for the pond edges. Succulent plants can solve the problem because they form dense and compact mats, so they can be chosen and planted up as a wonderful living carpet. They offer a variety of textures, shapes and colours and because many of the plants are evergreen, they can offer a year-round solution.

ABOVE *Delosperma nubigenum* with its lime-green foliage and bright yellow flowers in the spring makes a wonderful living edge to this pond

ABOVE *Sedum pachyclados* and saxifraga edge this pond, which also provides a home for frogs, newts and goldfish

CHOOSING YOUR PLANTS

Carpeting succulents can create a colourful, evergreen living edge to your pool, which will cover every scrap of liner and drip over into the water itself.

In the pond, keep to your architectural theme with rushes, sedges, and irises, which have the benefit of producing dramatic spiky foliage and a wide range of colourful flowers. At the damp edges of the pond itself you can cheat a little and go for spiky acorus. They are not true ornamental grasses but they are grass-like, with flattened fans of dark green leaves. Because they enjoy damp conditions they are very good for pond sides. Look out also for *Acorus gramineus* 'Variegatus', which is a hardy, perennial, semi-evergreen, with

RIGHT Textural and colourful *Sedum album f. murale* 'Coral Carpet' frames this waterfall

LEFT *Delosperma nubigenum* is a spring-flowering acid-green succulent 'carpet'

dark green and cream variegated arching foliage, reaching a height of 10in (25cm) and a spread of 6in (15cm).

For the edges of the pool you can choose from the following hardy, carpeting succulents: *Crassula alba* – rosette-forming, pointed, fleshy leaves with finely serrated edges, white flowers *Lewisia* hybrids – evergreen, clumping perennials with rosettes of dark leaves. In early summer they carry beautiful clusters of flowers in shades of pink. They are hardy but like good drainage *Delosperma cooperi* and *D. nubigenum* with mats of succulent leaves. *Delosperma cooperi* produces lilac-pink flowers all summer while *D. nubigenum* has yellow flowers in spring.

ABOVE **Vigorous-growing** *Sedum pachyclados,* **saxifraga and cushion-forming** *Scleranthus biflorus* **will completely cover the pond liner in no time**

ABOVE *Sedum spathulifolium* var. *purpureum* and *S. acre* 'Yellow Queen' are both evergreen mat-forming perennials

Sedums such as *Sedum acre* 'Yellow Queen', an evergreen, mat-forming perennial which has dense spreading shoots, clothed in tiny, fleshy, pale green leaves, variegated yellow and which bears abundant small yellow flowers

Sedum album f. *murale* 'Coral Carpet', with small rounded or cylindrical leaves, green, red and maroon, and small white flowers

Sedum album var. *micranthum* subvar. *chloroticum*, which has small, succulent leaves with white, starry flowers

Sedum x *amecamecanum*, with scrambling or trailing stems that are covered in silver and green rounded leaves and bearing small, yellow star-shaped flowers

Sedum anacampseros, which is a scrambling plant reaching 8in (20cm) long, and has tiny lower leaves, or otherwise bare lower stems, and elongating rosettes of leaves at the stem tips. It has lovely red-purple flowers, but it does not flower readily

Sedum cauticola 'Lidakense', tiny, grey-green succulent leaves, bearing rich dark red flowers

Sedum dasyphyllum, a low-growing, compact plant, only 1½in (4cm) high, with a mass of grey foliage and white flowers

Sedum divergens, which is column forming with spherical, succulent, shiny red and green leaves and yellow flowers

Sedum ellacombianum, has toothed green leaves and yellow flowers

Sedum ewersii 'Nanum' is a trailing perennial with attractive blue-grey leaves and red flowers

Sedum hispanicum is a mat-forming grey-green plant covered in miniature cylindrical leaves. Pink to white flowers cover the plant in summer

ABOVE **Ponds and gravel gardens go together particularly well**

ABOVE *Cleistocactus straussi* bedded out for the summer makes a fabulous frame to the pond

Sedum middendorffianum, which is mat-forming with green-brown leaves and striking yellow-orange spiky flowers

Sedum pachyclados is a mound-forming species with dark green leaves and lots of pinkish flowers

Sedum pluricaule is a spreading plant, with small grey-green leaves and dark red flowers

Sedum spathulifolium 'Cape Blanco' has flat rosettes of fleshy, silvery leaves and clusters of small yellow flowers

Sedum spathulifolium var. *purpureum* has flat rosettes of fleshy grey and purple leaves and clusters of small yellow flowers

Sedum spurium var. *variegatum* is a pretty, variegated, carpeting succulent, with green leaves edged with pink and with pink flowers

Crassula alba, is a rosette-forming plant with pointed, fleshy leaves with finely serrated edges and white flowers

Any of the sempervivums and jovibarbas will make effective edging for your pond.

Once you have clothed the edges of your pond, you will need to choose a sympathetic planting scheme to surround it. Yuccas are high-impact succulent plants and can look very striking alongside complementary architectural plants including cordylines and the hardy palms. Phormiums also relate particularly well to the spiky forms of the rushes, sedges, acorus and irises at the water's edge; you will also find that the colour palette combines well with the colours of carpeting succulents.

HOW TO KEEP IT LOOKING GOOD

Unfortunately, you cannot line the area carpeting the pond with membrane, as you want the plants to root well into the soil to bind the edges. Therefore you will have to make sure that the soil you are planting into is as weed-free as possible, and you will then need to weed meticulously thereafter.

But don't despair if you lose control of weeds. You can actually lift up the edging plants wholesale, strip out the weeds and re-lay them as living carpet tiles. The photograph below shows how a whole section of a garden has been lifted up in great chunks, which can then be re-established where, and when, required. Actually, this photograph should be captioned 'Why you should always use permeable membrane when you construct a gravel bed', because it marks the sorry end of our first gravel garden. Since then, membrane always goes down first.

You will also want to retain the careful balance of colours you have chosen – or improve on it if you haven't chosen as well as you hoped. You will find that, in time, one or two of the species will grow so vigorously as to overwhelm the others. In this case, you can literally pull away excess material. You can use it to fill in any gaps or to make alterations. Just make sure you have plenty of soil at the roots, water it well before replanting, and again, keep it back from the water's edge, to save fouling the water.

ABOVE **Weed-free succulents ready to be relaid through a permeable membrane which will suppress future weed growth**

CHAPTER 8

Carpet bedding

Carpet, or tapestry, bedding was much loved by the Victorians and Edwardians. The basic form is a geometrical shape subdivided into many symmetrical areas, with low-growing and contrasting plants picking out the outlines and the infilling.

This is the most formal approach in this kind of gardening; it is the equivalent of topiary or the use of box hedging in knot gardens. As a result, it is highly labour intensive and it requires large quantities of plants. 9ft^2 (3m^2)

requires about 500 plants and pro rata, so it is not to be undertaken lightly. However, if you restrict your choice to succulent plants, it will require much less watering and maintenance than some of the other spreading varieties which can be used, such as tanacetum, kleinia, alternathera or ajuga.

It is also fun and very satisfying to plan and execute, either on a small scale in simple geometrical patterns or in some huge scheme to celebrate an important birthday, for instance, or a birth or special anniversary.

SITING

Both the planting and its surroundings have to be immaculate and the siting is crucial. This kind of scheme needs to be well and truly visible, so consider insertion in a sloping bank, in a sunken area, in a position below a terrace, or perhaps under a window.

ABOVE **Before planting up, you must establish your centreline of plants, to ensure you have the symmetry that is essential to these schemes**

RIGHT **The cross of sempervivums goes in first to give accurate planting guidelines for the rest of the plants**

ABOVE **Echeverias are some of the best choices for carpet bedding**

PLANNING

This formal approach to gardening requries meticulous planning beforehand, so make a scale drawing of the bed. Graph paper and coloured pencils will be helpful and a compass, set square and protractor for those without a fatal aversion to maths would also help.

Try out a variety of schemes before you make a final choice, but for your first attempt, keep it fairly simple. Select a geometrical figure for an outline shape, e.g. a rectangle, which you can then subdivide into diamonds or smaller rectangles, and so on. You also need to decide whether your scheme is to be on one level or whether you want to have a three-dimensional effect with raised sections.

This is also in-your-face gardening. Go for strong contrast in colour and tone; the planting needs to be bold enough for the pattern to be clearly distinguishable; there's no place here for subtle harmonies.

LEFT **A completed carpet bedding scheme, constructed in a mini walled bed. Top left, clockwise:** *Echeveria dereceana, E. subsesillis, Sedum clavatum* **and** *E. derenbergii,* **divided by a cross of deep red sempervivum cultivars**

ABOVE For a 3-D effect, you can make a simple, mounded, central section, following a gently curving profile, with drainage material as a foundation

ABOVE A more complex raised central area can be constructed out of chicken wire and lined with membrane. This is then filled with drainage material and soil and the plants are pushed through the membrane and wire to cover the sides

When you have chosen your final scheme, size it up and draw it out – accurately – by pouring sand from a bottle or scraping the outlines with a sharp stick. You can use any straight-edged item for drawing straight lines, and a string attached to a cane will draw out circles or ovals.

If you have chosen a three-dimensional effect, you will need to build up some of the areas. Do this with care, because you do not want to spoil all your hard work with a landslide. Probably the easiest approach is to make a chicken wire outline, lined with membrane, almost like a giant

hanging basket. This is, in effect, a raised bed with drainage material in the base covered with gritty topsoil. The sides of the raised structure are, of course, part of the planting scheme and can be planted up by pushing the root ball through the wire and membrane into the soil. You can go for a halfway house by building up some sections with soil, following a gently curving profile, perhaps with some hard core as a foundation.

For a small scheme, you can lay your plants on the surface before setting them to ensure regularity and that you don't run out of material. You need plenty of plants – although they will grow and intermingle, you don't want to start off too sparsely. For a large scheme you will need to draw out your design to scale and plant it up in sections with a pre-planned quantity of plants for each section. As a rule of thumb, go for a 2in (5cm) spacing between the plants, and plant with care, as you want this to look as meticulous as possible.

If the prospect of producing or buying the quantities of plants needed is too daunting, you can use a number of cheats. You can subdivide

LEFT When you are planning a carpet bed on a small scale, you can arrange the plants on the surface, to make sure you have enough, and the effect is what you want. Here, contrasting sempervivums are used, with *Aloe aristata* as a centrepiece

ABOVE After you have checked the scheme, and made any alterations, you can then bed in the plants. This bed is made in a log roll, which is 8ft (2.5m) long and 6in (15cm) high, and the picture was taken one month after initial planting

ABOVE The tightly packed heads of *Echeveria gibbiflora* lend themselves to massed planting in blocks of colour

ABOVE **The pots of** *Echeveria secunda* **pictured here are in flower. However, unless you want a looser effect, it is best to take the buds off, to maintain your chosen colours and shapes**

ABOVE **This 'green roof' is ecologically sound and an attractive version of carpet bedding**

your infilled shapes with hard materials instead of more plants e.g. bricks, little paving stones, cobbles, etc. This also gives you a permanent framework for ringing the changes every year if you so wish.

CHOOSING YOUR PLANTS

For a simple one-plant scheme I suggest that you look at echeverias. These are also excellent choices for outlining the shapes before infilling with smaller plants.

For accent plants for the centrepiece features of a bed you could look at *Aeonium tabuliforme*, *A. arboreum*, *A. arboreum* 'Zwartkop' and *Agave americana* 'Variegata', plus other large agaves, *Aloe aristata*, cordyline and phormium.

It is essential to fill the beds, because the aim is to have complete ground cover as quickly as possible. With economy in mind, therefore, you may want to begin propagating the plants during the previous year to ensure that you have sufficient quantities. These ground-covering plants are all easy to propagate by taking off segments, drying them out for a couple of weeks and then setting them into a slightly damp and gritty compost.

LEFT **Jewel-like detail from the floral clock that is pictured at the bottom of the facing page**

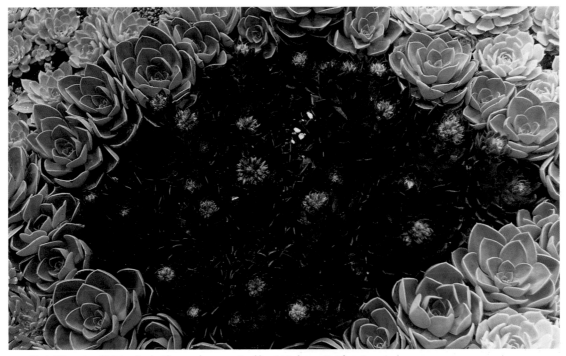

ABOVE Black *Echeveria affinis* is edged with strongly contrasting lilac *E.* 'Perle von Nurnberg'

HOW TO KEEP THEM LOOKING GOOD

A formal scheme such as this needs to look immaculate, so make sure it is weed-free.

Keep clipping the plants back if they threaten to grow into one another and muddy your outlines.Ensure your clipping is as precise as possible in order to preserve the demarcation lines between your blocks of pattern. You may find that secateurs or even scissors give you the most control in tight spaces, although you can use shears on larger areas (smaller-bladed ladies' models are ideal). Take away any cut material, as nothing looks worse than decaying plant material. Debud any plants that attempt to flower, as foliage effects give by far the cleanest lines. You do not want these plants to flower and spoil the solid blocks of colour. Keep some spares back to infill if you have any casualties.

If you really get the bug, start planning ahead for next year's even grander scheme (a clock or your coat of arms?) by propagating the plants you will need in plenty of time.

ABOVE This section from a wonderful floral clock at the Chelsea Flower Show, London, south England, designed by Edinburgh City Council shows a classic use of succulents in colourful carpet bedding

79

CHAPTER 9

Care and maintenance

Although these are easy plants to care for, you need to cultivate a hard heart if your plants are to really thrive. Forget all your preconceptions: traditionally, house and conservatory plants are a constant worry, regarded as always in need of water, food or both. We are instructed to keep a moist microclimate around the plants by standing them in trays filled with pebbles and water in order to create a constant humidity, and the last thing we should ever do is let the compost dry out completely. If a plant wilts, its condition is often terminal, so a sickly plant is generally treated with water – and that means plenty of it.

Now, however, you must forget all of those rules. Cacti and other succulents are more likely to die from over-zealous care than for any other reason, so you will need to develop a culture of benign neglect. Don't worry even if your plants appear to shrivel slightly: they will be magically resurrected as soon as they receive water.

COMPOSTS

Succulents will thrive in any normal houseplant compost, whether it is a multipurpose mix or John Innes soil-based or a loam-based compost, numbers 2 or 3. Soilless multipurpose composts are lightweight, so you may find that pots containing taller plants will topple over when they are due to be watered. The advantage of this compost, however, is that you can easily knock the root ball out of the pot to examine the root system for pests, and the whole plant can be turned out and put back into its pot without any mess or compost loss. Soil-based composts are heavier, so your pots will remain more stable, but if you invert the pot all the compost will cascade out and the plant will need repotting. If you suspect that you will be heavy-handed with watering, add horticultural grit to the mix to improve drainage – although in this case you will have a landslide when you come to upend the pot, whichever compost you use.

All of these plants should be completely dry before they are next watered. Don't, however, go to the opposite extreme of potting your plants in sand and neglecting to water them at all. True, they won't die, but they certainly won't look very attractive, either.

Once the compost is dry, the plants should be given a generous drenching and then allowed to dry out again. You will find that the plants are being watered once a week in the summer, possibly twice if it is very sunny. However, if you are in any doubt about watering, don't. The plants won't suffer, and it is safer to water too little than too much. Although containers can look very pretty with a top dressing of gravel, this does mean that you can't tell whether the compost has dried out or not: until you are used to succulents, keep at least one or two pots free of top-dressing, so that you can check on their condition more easily.

When the plants are in full growth they appreciate regular feeding every four weeks or so. There are special formulations for cacti, such as Chempak cactus and succulent fertilizer, which has a specially balanced NPK (nitrogen, phosphorus, potassium) formulation of 8-34-32. Having said this, you will find that high-potassium fertilizers will also suit cacti and other succulents: 15-15-30, perhaps, or similar fertilizers formulated for tomatoes, such as NPK 10-10-25 or 11-9-30. A balanced NPK will do no harm, however, so the most indolent solution is to mix a little granulated slow-release fertilizer with a 20-20-20 formulation into the compost when you first pot up the plants.

WHEN TO WATER

You can grow a wide range of plants in either an unheated or frost-free conservatory, as long as the plants are completely dry over the winter. An unheated conservatory is often effectively the same as one kept just above freezing (about 4°C/40°F), as the borrowed heat from the house is usually enough to keep the temperature that bit higher than it would be in a greenhouse.

In the autumn, gradually reduce watering until, by end of autumn, your plants are completely dry. They will then stay bone-dry until the spring when, from early spring onwards, you should very gradually start up the watering again to bring the plants back into growth. This is the most critical stage for cacti, as too much water too soon may cause them to rot, so let the pot dry out completely between waterings.

You will be able to clearly see when the plants are producing new growth: in a globular cactus, for instance, a tightly packed fur of new spines appears in the growing point or points of the plants, and the whole plant becomes a little bit plumper.

ABOVE **This echeveria attacked by mould is a sorry victim of overwatering**

ABOVE **An unusual pest – a leaf cutter bee has made its nest in the damp compost of this pot**

ABOVE **This aloe has 'die-back' at the leaf tips, caused by excessive dryness**

This dry period is necessary in order to protect the plants during the winter. The plants are literally smaller in the winter, as they will have shrunk into themselves to protect their structures. This dormancy is also essential for bud formation, and a failure to provide it is one of the most common reasons for flowering to fail.

Once your plants have reached the necessary size they should flower like clockwork every year, as long as they have had their winter snooze. They generally flower in the spring or early summer. The rebutias, mammillarias, lobivias, notocactus, epiphyllums (orchid cacti) and Christmas cacti are particularly good for flowers, and some will bloom more than once in the same year.

The treatment of your cacti and other succulents indoors or in a heated conservatory is necessarily rather different. The plants still need to have a drier resting period, but they won't go into the kind of suspended animation that they would adopt in the colder conditions of a space kept just above freezing. In warmer conditions you will need to give your plants an occasional light watering or misting from time to time to prevent them shrivelling. This applies especially to the other succulents, which may well carry on growing, although more slowly, throughout the winter. Some of the crassulas will also delight you with masses of tiny white flowers – very welcome in the winter months. Keep all cacti (except Christmas or Holiday cacti) as dry as possible, with a light watering if they appear too desiccated. The other succulents require similar care, although, in general, they need less sun and a little more water, and they are rather more vigorous in their growth. Lithops are the notable exception, relishing a sunny position and hating too much water.

Cacti and other succulents make attractive all-year-round houseplants, because you will find that their appearance won't change very much during the colder months.

REPOTTING

As your plants grow and change they will need to be moved into larger containers, with fresh nutrient-rich compost and room for the roots to spread. With most of your plants this is straightforward. Choose a clean pot, the next size up from the one your plant is in, fill it loosely with compost and push the smaller pot down into it to make an outline of the space the root ball will need. Dislodge the plant from the container by turning it upside-down and tapping it sharply on the side of a bench, shelf or table.

Take this opportunity to have a really good look at the root ball, to make sure that there is no damage or infestation. If you find mealy bugs, remove all the compost from the roots and dispose of it well away from any other plants. Dip the plant in an insecticide, such as imidacloprid, before potting the plant up in clean, new compost. Take a look at the plants surrounding the infested one in case the pests

SAFETY
You may be slightly baffled when you look at a really prickly cactus, wondering how you can put it into a larger pot without the danger of harming yourself. Damage limitation methods include the obvious one of wearing stout gloves. You may, however, be surprised how spines can penetrate even the toughest material.

There is another, cunning alternative approach which avoids damage to you or the plant. Take a page of newspaper and fold it over and over until it makes a firm, long, thin rectangular strip. Put this around the plant, and pinch the two ends of the strip together with your finger and thumb, close to the plant body, creating a handle to hold. You will find that you will have a circular collar surrounding the plant, which you can hold gently but firmly enough for you to be able to upend the pot and tap it to loosen the plant as described above. Still using your handle, you can then place the plant in its new container and firm it in with no harm to either of you.

Children are often fascinated by cacti, yet the spines can be fierce and some have a horrible fish-hook feature, so it is easy for little fingers – and pets' noses – to get damaged. If you have children or pets, therefore, do please keep your spikiest plants, such as the cacti and some of the agaves with their terminal spines, well out of their reach. The agave spines can also be cut off, using scissors or secateurs, with no harm whatsoever to the plant.

RIGHT **A handle made of newspaper keeps sharp spines at bay**

ABOVE **Mealy bugs nesting on a *Crassula lactea* leaf** and BELOW a trichocereus

have begun to spread. If this is the case, then it is important to give those plants a dose of insecticide, too.

Nice, clean plants may simply have the stale compost teased from around their roots, with the plant being dropped into the pot while new compost is gently firmed in around it. Let the plant settle for a day or two, then start watering again, beginning with lower quantities than normal until the plant has had time to recover.

PESTS AND DISEASES

Basic hygiene, both in the house and the conservatory, involves removing dead leaves and the debris of flowers and other material which gathers around the pots: this helps avoid fungal infection. You can leave flowers on, in which case they often form attractive, colourful seed pods and will possibly give you your own seed to experiment with. It is, however, safe to remove them if you prefer a tidier plant. Just wait until they are completely dead and dry, when you can rub them away.

Unfortunately, in an artificial environment such as a conservatory you cannot rely on the normal checks and balances to keep pests under control, so you will need to keep your eyes open for insect pests. On the whole, plants that are well looked after are much less susceptible to attack. Luckily, you won't find masses of blackfly, greenfly or whitefly disfiguring your plants (except possibly your aeoniums), because these plants don't have the soft leaves which aphids love. Pyrethrum-based insecticides, and those based on natural fatty acids, are effective but short-lived contact insecticides. These include Bio Organic Pest Control, Greenfingers Organics Pest Spray, Doff Houseplant Pest Spray and Growing Success Bug Killer. For serious infestations use an insecticide containing imidacloprid, such as Bio Provado Ultimate Bug Killer and Bio Provado Vine Weevil Killer. This new type of insecticide is highly systemic, but also has a contact killing action.

ABOVE **This mammillaria is rotting from the inside out as a result of too much water, too much cold, or both**

MEALY BUGS
(PSEUDOCOCCUS SPECIES)

These look a bit like woodlice in shape, but they have a protective waxy white coating, so you will see these as white, woolly tufts, about ½in (1–3mm) long, which are tucked into inaccessible corners of leaf joints, camouflaged in the wool around spines and so on. These are generally slow-moving, sucking parasites which can be removed individually In a small infestation by dabbing them with methylated spirits on a cotton wool bud.

ROOT MEALY BUGS
(RHIZOECUS SPECIES)

These are a much greater pest, because they are completely hidden from view while feasting on the roots, causing stunting or failure of the

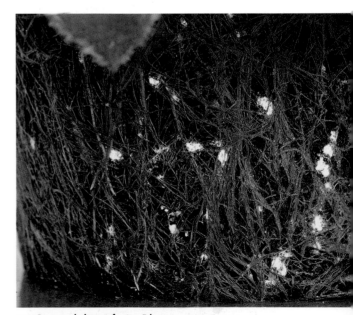

ABOVE **Root mealy bugs infesting *Echeveria setosa***

LEFT This dark-bodied neoporteria shows typical damage inflicted by sap-sucking red spider mites

plant. For this reason you will need to turn the plant out of the pot from time to time to check for telltale white tufts among the roots and compost. This is the argument for a soilless multipurpose compost, because you can examine the root ball and pop the plant straight back into its pot without having to repot it. You can use the same cotton wool bud remedy as above, but there is a case for removing compost from the roots, dunking the plant in Provado Vine Weevil Killer and repotting it in fresh compost.

SCALE INSECTS (DACTYLOPIUS CACTI)

These can be cactus lovers: indeed, they are grown commercially on opuntias for cochineal,

CHEMICAL-FREE CONTROL

If you are unhappy about the use of toxic chemicals in close proximity to your living space, you may be interested in the use of diatomaceous earth, which is made from the skeletal remains of minute algae.

Traditionally used in water filtration processes, this completely inert material can be used at a rate of a 1 tbsp (15ml) to 1¾ pint (1 litre) of soil. It destroys mealy bugs in an elegant, if gruesome, manner: the remains of the algae are reduced to needle-sharp particles which are believed to shred the bodies of small soil-inhabiting insects.

There is also a non-toxic, biodegradable substance derived from the oil of the neem tree (*Asadirachta indica*), a native of Burma and India where it is traditionally known as

'the village pharmacy'. Neem tree oil is non-toxic and biodegradable and is believed to have insecticidal and fungicidal properties. It is used in a solution of one ounce (30ml) of oil to a gallon (4.5 litres) of water, together with an equal amount of soft soap.

If you can bring yourself to live with plants which are not entirely pest free, then you might try to achieve a natural balance by using biological controls. Ladybirds will attack mealy bugs and scale insects, while syrphid flies and lacewings live on mealy bugs. However, it can be difficult to maintain the balance between predators and their prey in a small-scale collection. For example there is a wasp *Encarsia formosa* which lays eggs in immature whitefly and kills them – but the wasps need a constant supply of whitefly or they will also die.

the red dye. (There are other culprits, such as *Pinnaspis aspidistrae* and *Coccus hesperidum*.) They can be seen as small spots about 1/16–1/4in (2–6mm) in diameter, which cling on in a limpet-like manner: these are the females, which have a protective shell to protect them while they suck sap and lay their eggs. Low-grade infestations can be treated with methylated spirits or soapy water on a cotton wool bud or paintbrush.

SAP-SUCKING RED SPIDER MITES (TETRANYCHUS SPECIES)

Almost invisible to the naked eye, they are about 1/1000in (0.02mm) across and usually look like tiny orange dots, although they can be other colours too, and they are always surrounded by a very fine webbing. Treatment must be rapid, as this is a pest which can spread quickly. These bugs are susceptible to insecticides containing butoxycarboxim. If you dislike chemical treatments, you can mist the plants and open windows as a deterrent, because this is a bug of dry conditions and poor ventilation. You can also use neem tree oil, as described in the panel on the left.

SCIARID FLY (SCIARIDAE)

A pest of wet, peat-based compost, the sciarid fly is a problem, especially when seedlings are being raised, so these bugs are dealt with in Chapter 10, Propagation.

FUNGAL INFECTION

This is often an indicator of poor hygiene, because these infections will only develop in the kind of damp conditions to which cacti and other succulents should never be subjected. Fortunately, it is possible to treat infected plants with a proprietary copper-based fungicide.

ABOVE **Natural control in action – this ladybird is guzzling on whitefly**

BELOW **This echeveria is being attacked by mould; if you cut off the damaged material and keep the plant dry it stands a good chance of recovery**

CHAPTER 10

Propagation

One of the big bonuses of any kind of gardening is propagating extra plants of your own at little or no cost. By using your existing plants as material to be cannibalized, you can make an impact on those blank spaces much more rapidly than you perhaps imagined.

Cacti and other succulents provide the opportunity for a variety of approaches, from taking offsets and cuttings, through to grafting and to growing plants from your own seed.

OFFSETS

Fortunately the clustering cacti will reproduce themselves in miniature as part of their normal habit of growth, and these offsets are perfect replicas of the parent plant. You can, of course, allow the original to grow on and develop into a wonderful multi-headed specimen. However, in the summer months when the plant is growing so vigorously that both the parent and its offsets will recover rapidly, you can choose to take some or all of the babies away from the parent,

ABOVE **An offset of *Mammillaria zeilmanniana* with roots developing**

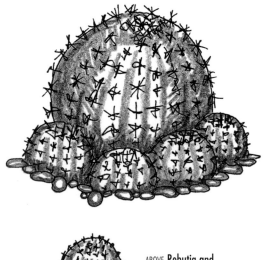

ABOVE **Rebutia and offset** (LEFT)

ABOVE **You can increase your collection by all sorts of methods, including taking cuttings, grafting and removing offsets and seeds**

potting them on to grow into larger plants. The extra space and nourishment now available to the mother plant means it will grow more quickly than if left intact.

Many of the globular cacti, such as rebutias, echinopsis, chamaecereus, lobivias and mammillarias, are freely offsetting, and even some of the rarer genera will often clump up readily, too. Notocactus are unusual in that, although they offset readily, they often reproduce underground. To find the offsets, probe through the soil gently with your fingertips until you find their hiding places.

You may find that once you have taken the plant out of its pot, you can separate the offsets by tugging them gently apart. If you are lucky you will also find you have a tiny root system, in which case you can immediately pot up the 'pup'

ABOVE **Agave and offset in the compost.** LEFT **Offset on its own**

89

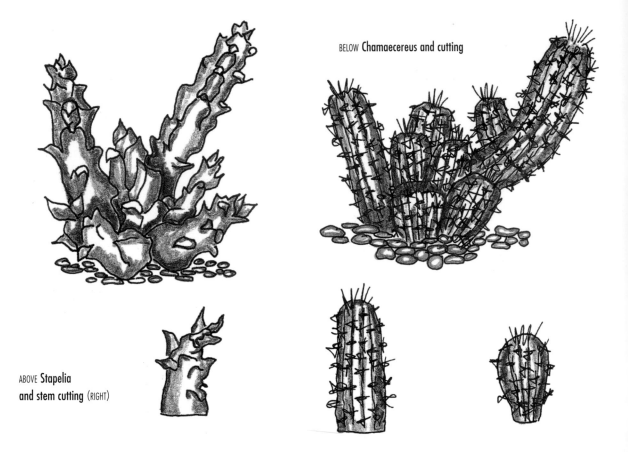

BELOW **Chamaecereus and cutting**

ABOVE **Stapelia
and stem cutting** (RIGHT)

into any houseplant compost. You have a choice between John Innes soil-based compost (numbers 1 or 2), a peat-based compost, which will benefit from the addition of a little gravel, or any of the new, coir-based or multipurpose variants, again with the addition of a little gravel.

Sometimes you have to be a little more ruthless and cut the offset away from the parent with a clean, sharp knife. Put the offset to one side in a dry, shady place for the cut surface to callous over. This will take about a week to ten days, and then you can pot the plant up in the same mixture as for the ready-rooted offset described above.

Any of the readily clumping and clustering succulents, such as faucarias, lithops and conophytums, can be treated in the same way.

Separate them gently, just as with the cacti. If they have been cut, you will need to wait a week to ten days, but otherwise you can pot them up straight away.

Some succulents, such as agaves and aloes, produce offsets on thickened runners which develop in the root system. You will find these baby plants appearing around and under the rosettes, although you can also often find them under the surface when you are repotting the plants. A bowl or cauldron-shaped container with curved sides is good for these plants, as it seems to encourage the offsets to head to the surface quickly. These baby plants can be detached gently from the parent plant and potted up immediately, because they already have their own root systems.

CUTTINGS

Because some plants are much less obliging, you will have to take things into your own hands if you want to produce extra plants as quickly as you can. Your cuttings should be taken during the growing season. Late spring and early summer are the best times, and all propagation should ideally be done between early spring and early autumn. It is certainly possible to take cuttings in the autumn, but in this case they are best left unpotted until the following spring: if they are in a dry position they will amaze you with their ability to survive in a kind of suspended animation, and when you eventually come to pot them up you may well find that roots are already beginning to form.

An essential tool when taking cuttings is a clean, sharp and, preferably, unserrated knife. You also need some clean, dry, empty plant saucers or seed trays, in which you can place the cut material in a dry and shaded position while it dries out. Hygiene is essential. Dirt and moisture harbour all sorts of moulds, bacteria and pests which might infect your plant material. Ideally you should also thoroughly clean the blade between each cutting to prevent a possible spread of infection.

STEM CUTTINGS

Taking stem cuttings is a form of vegetative propagation. The plants that you grow from the cuttings will be identical to the parents, and this can be vital if some feature, such as variegation, cannot be perpetuated in any other way. Interestingly, variegation in a plant cannot be reproduced by leaf cuttings: there has to be some stem involved or the plant will be the self-green of the original species again.

Cuttings should be taken at a natural joint if possible – from the side or base in the case of a branching cactus, or a stem or pad in a jointed species. Most cacti and many fleshy stemmed succulents can be propagated like this. This is also a good way to increase some of the exotic-flowering cacti, such as the epiphyllums, aporocactus and selenicereus, all of which root readily as stem cuttings. However, if you cut the stem into several pieces, do remember to mark the bottom end: it is often hard to tell which end is which, but it is really important to pot them up the right way in the compost.

Take great care with euphorbia cuttings, as all of these plants have a milky and irritant sap. If you begin taking your cuttings from the bottom of the plant and work your way upwards you can avoid a lot of trouble, because by doing this the sap will not drip on you as you continue to take your cuttings. Watering the stock plant afterwards will remove most of the white sap. I would suggest that you always wear gloves with euphorbias, and that you wash your hands well after taking cuttings of any plant.

It may sound ruthless, but you can take your cutting straight across a stem. The plant will look very sorry for itself, but the top part can be rooted to form a perfect new plant and the cut surface will sprout several new pieces which can then be detached in turn to make new plants

ABOVE *Cotyledon orbiculata* stem cutting with roots forming

ABOVE AND LEFT **An *Opuntia subulata*** before and after cutting.
The lower part will often sprout to form a majestic candelabrum

or left where they are so that they can produce a branching plant. *Opuntia subulata* and other columnar plants such as cereus and cleistocactus can be treated like this, and the resulting parent plant can become a really striking candelabrum in time. In the case of padded opuntias you can remove a pad (again, this will trigger the parent to produce more than one pad to replace it) or you can take off a side branch.

As well as increasing your stock, taking cuttings is a way of managing plants. They can be used to rescue a diseased plant if you cut off a healthy part well above the diseased or damaged section. You can also tidy up lopsided or top-heavy growth, or behead a columnar plant that is outgrowing its space: a new, smaller plant will be established, while the cut portion will resprout into a more compact multi-headed plant. A cutting will often grow away with much more vigour than the parent plant, which may have been slowing down.

Take a bit of time before you start sawing away at your plants. Look for the most suitable area to separate the cutting from the host plant, and make it a smooth, even cut, without any rough

ABOVE **Adromischus leaf cutting: plant and roots forming**

ABOVE **Echeveria leaf cutting: new plant and roots appearing**

edges. Put the cutting into a clean container in a dry and shady place, perhaps tucked under a conservatory shelf, where it should remain to dry out for a week or so, erring on the side of more rather than less time. Its progress depends on both the temperature and the time of year, as a cutting will be ready sooner in the middle of the growing season and when the temperatures are higher. This isn't rocket science, however, and you won't court certain failure if you pot a cutting up a bit too soon. If you are really worried, just wait until you see the tiny new roots appearing: pot your cutting up at this point and success is virtually guaranteed.

You may be experienced at taking cuttings of 'normal' house and garden plants, but remember that, unlike most other plants, cacti actually dislike being too wet. These are the last plants to root up by standing them in a glass of water. Because cacti and other succulents lack the resistance to bacteria and moisture-borne fungal infections which plants originating in wetter areas possess, they fall prey to these attacks very readily. Keep them dry, and they will often surprise you by producing tiny roots even before you come to pot them up.

After a week or two, pot them up into slightly moist compost. Any houseplant compost will do (multipurpose, peat-based with extra gravel or soil-based), but they will appreciate a gritty mix, which you can give them by adding a generous handful of horticultural grit or sharp sand – just think how quickly weed seedlings will root in garden gravel beds which have no weed suppression membrane in place. Water the cuttings really sparingly until they show signs of growth, when you can build up watering until you are giving them water and feed as usual.

LEAF CUTTINGS

Many succulents, among them echeverias, crassulas, kalanchoes and sedums, can be propagated quickly and easily by removing a leaf from the parent plant. Choose a plump healthy leaf and allow it to dry out, just as with the stem cuttings. You will find that a whole new miniature plant will develop from the base of the leaf, which will eventually shrivel away.

Rosette-forming succulents can be set with a small piece of stem still attached. Aeoniums can be propagated by taking one of the rosettes which form its crown.

ROOT CUTTINGS

If you look at the root system of yuccas and agaves you will sometimes see a very thick branching which is distinctly different from the normal, thinner and more fibrous appearance. Cut off pieces of this engorged root, allowing the sections to dry out, and you will be rewarded with a new crop of plants. The pieces should be at least 2in (5cm) long, and they should preferably have some small roots on them

ABOVE **A root cutting of yucca, with new plants developing**

already. With time, complete new plantlets will form from these pieces, sometimes with the additional bonus of more than one per section. Once a plantlet has developed its own roots, cut it off at the parent root, pot it up in the usual mixture and then gradually build up your watering regime as before.

COLLECTING YOUR OWN SEED

Many of the cacti genera make a dazzling display of flowers in the spring and early summer, and then go on to set seed, while some other succulents, such as the autumn-flowering lithops, will also set seed readily. Keep an eye on the ripening pods, which should be removed from the plant once they are ripe and the mature seed is black and hard. Your motto should always be: the fresher the seed the better. To remove the seedpods is also to practise good hygiene, because those left on over the winter are not only a focus for rot and decay, but they are also all too susceptible to raids by hungry mice. Having said that, however, plants such as

LEFT **These highly attractive seed pods of *Ceropegia woodii* will soon be ready to remove from the plant**

ABOVE *Setiechinopsis mirabilis* freshly in bud . . .

RIGHT . . . and with the bud well developed

mammillarias and rhipsalis have such pretty fruits that aesthetics can sometimes outweigh good housekeeping.

Pods of some species will split open easily, and the ripe seed will cascade out ready for sowing. Rebutias will flower readily in the spring, quickly fruit and also provide ripe seed which can be germinating by mid-summer.

Some seed pods, such as mammillarias, are fleshy. To remove this seed, squash the pod then soak it well in a jar of water. You will be able to see the heavier seed separate from the pulp, dropping to the base of the container while the debris floats above it. Lithops have seemingly impenetrable seed pods, and can fox attempts to get into them. The trick here is to give them literally a drop of water, and the pods will peel open magically to reveal a really fine, dust-like seed. Don't sneeze!

Of course, some species will hybridize very readily. This can be exciting with, for instance, epiphyllum or chamaecereus, which may give you your own choice hybrid with fabulous flower coloration; you can control the outcome by selecting likely parents. Epiphyllum growers have produced a cornucopia of beautifully coloured hybrids by this method. There is also scope with some of the other small, easily flowering globular cacti, like rebutias and sulcorebutias, and these include inter-genera hybrids such as crosses between lobivia and echinopsis.

95

ABOVE *Mammilaria bombycina* with ripe seed pods which are ready for harvesting

LEFT *Setiechinopsis mirabilis* seed pod opened to show a mass of ripe seed ready for collection

If you want your new plants to be true to the parent plant, you need to stop insects from reaching the flowers. Use a new, clean paintbrush to cross-pollinate those you have chosen.

To ensure that no intruder can sabotage your work, it is always a good idea to place a polythene bag over each one after pollination. Hold the bag in position with an elastic band around the mouth, and then make sure that you label it with the details of its 'father'; this is especially important if you are trying to produce interesting crosses.

SEEDLING DEVELOPMENT

It is very exciting to watch the development of your seedlings from tiny beginnings to the day they come into flower. If you are lucky, this will

take about 18 months, but two or three years is more usual and some types take even longer. Sow your seed in spring or summer, unless you have access to a lighted and heated propagator – in which case you can set them at any time.

SEED-RAISING

I have tried many methods of seed-raising at the nursery, and the following comes out tops. Use new, clean, plastic pots, about 3in (7.5cm) in diameter, for your sowings. Loosely fill them, almost to the top, with a John Innes soil-based seed compost. Use a fine sieve to sprinkle on the final ¼in (5mm) of compost, to give this layer a really open texture.

Using a sprayer, or a watering can with a fine rose, water the pot until all the compost is wet. Allow a few seconds between waterings so the water has time to sink in and doesn't wash the compost out of the pot. Alternatively, you can soak the pots by standing them in a container of water. After it settles, you will find that the

ABOVE Cacti and other succulent seeds vary enormously, like the plants themselves. Here we see opuntia species and *Delosperma hirtum* seeds. Both are actual size

ABOVE A heap of seed-raising mix (2 parts John Innes seed compost; 1 part sharp fine gravel; 1 part sharp sand) together with the equipment needed for the job – hand sprayer, pots, sieve, tray for pots, polythene bags and plant labels

compost will be a short distance below the top of the pot. Next, insert a plastic label in the middle of the pot, so that it protrudes a good way above the top.

BELOW Stages of seedling development

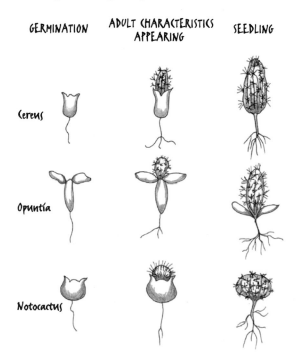

GERMINATION   ADULT CHARACTERISTICS APPEARING   SEEDLING

Cereus

Opuntia

Notocactus

Sprinkle your seeds evenly over the surface of the compost. If you have a sprayer available (a small hand-type is ideal), wet the seeds with a fine spray of water. Despite the drought resistance of these plants, germination cannot take place unless the compost remains moist. For added protection, a fungicide such as Benlate may be added to the spray.

Cover the top of the pot with a transparent polythene sandwich bag and secure it with an elastic band around the rim of the pot. The label

ABOVE The first task is to fill the pots and soak the compost all the way through

97

ABOVE Once the labels have been pushed into the compost, the seeds are sown (small ones on top, larger ones to their own depth) and a hand sprayer is used to soak the seeds — either with plain water or with a fungicide mix

ABOVE Micro climate: the pots are covered with polythene bags secured with elastic bands, the central label preventing the bag from collapsing on to the seeds

will prevent the bag from collapsing on to the seeds. The seedlings need protection in their first, most vulnerable weeks when they are susceptible to attack by sciarid fly, fungus gnats or mushroom flies – which are the same as the ubiquitous fruit flies which plague your wine glass or fruit bowl in the summer. These nuisances don't normally cause much of a problem, because they feed on decaying organic debris, but they will certainly damage tiny seedlings. Adult flies can be trapped by hanging up one of those yellow sticky flypaper strips, but this is not much help when the maggots are already there, sealed in a polythene bag with your seedlings. You can use a simple spray, like a Baby Bio houseplant spray or you can water the soil with a proprietary fungicide before setting the seeds. However, there shouldn't be a problem as long as you keep the bag in position and make absolutely sure that you have avoided using a peat-based compost, since this is a particularly good medium for these pests to thrive in. Again the best insecticides to use are the Bio Provado range containing imidacloprid, which will control sciarid fly for a year.

Place the pot in a warm place – a temperature of about 70°F (20°C) is ideal, although some fluctuation in temperature (plus or minus 10°F/ 5° or 6°C) will do no harm. Darkness is not required for germination, and the best position for the seeds will be well lit but out of intense sunlight. If the light is strong, cover your pot and polythene bag with a sheet of newspaper laid loosely over the top. Intense sunlight will make your seedlings go red, and their rate of growth will be greatly reduced. If the only warm place available to you is the airing cupboard then by all means use that, although you must be prepared for germination to be less successful. Give the seedlings light as soon as they have germinated.

What you are doing is giving the seeds the environment they would enjoy in their natural habitat, where they germinate against the base of the parent plant, shaded from the worst of the sun in the most moist position. Even if you don't bother to set seeds, you will sometimes find little seedlings appearing of their own accord under, say, the fat-bellied shelter of a globular cactus in one of your pots – an interesting illustration of their natural behaviour in the wild.

ABOVE At six months these seedlings are well advanced – rebutia species in the foreground and echinocereus at the back

After germination a temperature of 50°F (10°C) is required, but 70°F (20°C) or more will produce faster growth. Ideally, the seedlings should be left in their bags for about two months, and during this time the compost should remain moist. If it does dry out, stand the pot in a container of water until the top of the compost is wet again. It is very important, however, to check the bags regularly: if there are any problems with moss, fungal growth or stretching of the seedlings towards the light, the seedlings will be safer with the bags removed. After the polythene bags have been discarded, keep the compost slightly moist, either by standing the pots in a tray of water for a few minutes or by gentle spraying from above.

ABOVE These large and healthy seedlings of *Setiechinopsis mirabilis* are well on their way to maturity

99

Once the seedlings show spines they can be pricked out, but this is best left for a year after sowing unless there is severe overcrowding or some other problem arises. Mild overcrowding seems to have no detrimental effects: indeed, it is probably beneficial to the development of the seedlings, perhaps because it creates a favourable microclimate. If you prick them out too soon their growth seems to slow down dramatically. Don't prick out seedlings after late summer: it is far better to wait until the late spring of the following year. In the autumn, gradually

ABOVE *Pereskia aculeata* is commonly used for grafting seedlings

reduce watering and keep the seedlings dry from late autumn until early spring. Gentle watering may be resumed after this. During winter keep the plants in a well-lit position and don't allow the temperature to fall below about 40°F (5°C). Although some seedlings will withstand lower temperatures, experimentation can be dangerous.

Once your seedlings have started into growth in the spring that follows sowing, you can feel confident that they will reach maturity.

GRAFTING

Grafting is a more complicated method of plant propagation, and an operation for the more enthusiastic grower, but it is an engrossing process and can be a useful technique for a variety of reasons. Some cacti, especially the rare and choice varieties such as aztekium, pelecyphora and blossfeldia, are very slow-

LEFT Cristate and monstrous plants, like this fine specimen of *Myrtillocactus geometrizans* var. *monstrosus*, often grow much more vigorously when they are grafted onto a stronger stock

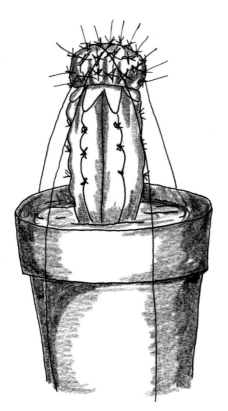

BELOW **The top of the seedling is severed from its own roots**

ABOVE **A slender pereskia stem with the top removed becomes a stock for a tiny seedling**

ABOVE **The trichocereus stock is chamfered (see page 103) with a gymnocalycium. Elastic bands hold the graft in place**

would not stand a chance of growing if they were not grafted on a green stock for chlorophyll production.

The unusual wavy and crested forms of cristate plants, which have developed as a result of physical, viral or genetic damage to the growing point, fascinate many people and often grow better when grafted. Some people also use this technique to create a 'standard' Christmas or holiday cactus, in the way that gardeners produce standard roses.

The best time for grafting is when plants are in strong growth, and once again the late spring and early summer is the most favoured time for trying this technique.

growing and can take an excessively long time to reach maturity if grown on their own roots. Grafting them as seedlings can accelerate their growth. The grafted plant is likely to become more engorged, and it will often produce many offsets. It can be left indefinitely to grow as a composite grafted plant, or it can be taken off the stock plant and treated as a cutting when it has grown big enough. This technique is also used to rescue a damaged or diseased specimen, which can often be saved by grafting a healthy part on to a stock plant.

Grafting also allows the growing of forms not found in nature. The Japanese, for example, have spent many years developing a range of gymnocalyciums without chlorophyll in shades of pinks, creams and maroons. These oddities

LEFT **A cactus spine attaches the seedling to the stock, which will supply all its nutrients once the graft has taken**

ABOVE **Red *Gymnocalycium damsii* grafted on trichocereus stock**

Success rates can be lower than in other methods of propagation, so it is probably wise to try to take several grafts at the same time in the hope that at least a few of them will prove to be successful.

The scion is the cutting or seedling which is to be grafted, and the vigorous rooted host plant is called the stock. A cactus plant obtains food and nutrients through vascular tissue: this can be seen in cross-section when a cactus stem is sliced through. It looks like a slightly darker core in the centre of the stem, surrounded by a circle of cells which act as water-storing tissue. For a graft to take, the vascular tissue in both the stock and scion has to be in contact in at least one place: the larger the areas in contact, the more successful the graft is likely to be. Ideally the stock plant should be a sturdy, fast-growing cactus, such as trichocereus or pereskia. A youngish, vigorous plant, a year or so old, is the best choice, and the stock should be at least as wide or ideally a bit wider than the scion. Again, aim for absolute cleanliness, using a clean, sharp knife, and cleaning it between operations.

In flat grafting both the stock and the scion should be cut straight across in a clean cut, with the edges of both pieces chamfered to fit together so as to avoid shrinkage.

Look carefully at the stock and the scion for the vascular rings. These should be lined up as far as possible, because this is where the plants will bond together. Try to avoid any air pockets forming between the two cut sections by gently rotating the pieces before finally fixing them. The two pieces should be held together firmly with crossed-over elastic bands or string going over the top of the scion and down underneath the pot. Some people use cocktail sticks or long cactus spines to hold the union together. This sounds more complicated than it is, but the illustrations below will make it clearer.

Trichocereus is the best genus to use as a stock for larger plants. For tiny seedlings look for the slender stems of pereskia, which are more in proportion to the scion.

In the case of long, slender scions – as, for example, when you are grafting a thin, columnar cactus – use a diagonal graft. The stock and the scion are cut on the diagonal and married together, joining them across the maximum possible surface area.

Keep the pot in a bright position, but out of full sun, for two to three weeks, after which the graft should have taken and the bands can be removed. Protect from full sun until the scion shows obvious signs of growth, when the plant can be treated just like any other member of your collection.

The other method of grafting is to use a cleft graft. This is the method of choice for plants like Christmas cacti and epiphyllums, which have a softer structure and which will give very small cut surfaces. In this case the stock has a V-shaped cut made into it, and the flat scion is tapered to shape and pushed down into the cleft to a depth of about 1in (2.5cm). The stock and scion are held together with a

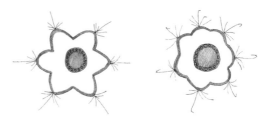

ABOVE **The cut surfaces of the scion and trichocereus stock, and the vascular tissue which needs to be aligned**

long spine or a cocktail stick. Cleft grafts need a little longer to take than flat grafts: allow a week or so more, and give them a shadier position. The composite plant is then treated in exactly the same way as described for the flat graft method.

Do not water any of your grafted plants until you are certain that the graft has taken. Again, if in doubt, wait for a longer rather than shorter period every time.

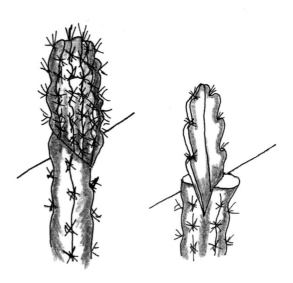

ABOVE LEFT **Diagonal graft**

ABOVE RIGHT **Cleft grafting Christmas cactus**

CHAPTER 11

A–Z plant directory

There is such an enormous range of cacti and other succulents for you to choose from that it is impossible to cover it all. This plant directory aims to cover a wide variety of attractive and interesting genera, offering a good choice of plants for you to use both indoors and out. And if you fall in love with a particular genus, if you follow it up you will find that there are usually many more species and cultivars for you to collect. Happy hunting!

THE NAMING OF PLANTS

Plants are grouped, or classified, according to common characteristics. The names that they are given indicate to which group they belong. The largest grouping, based on the structure of the plant's flowers, fruits and other organs, is the family. The family is then divided into genera and the genera into species.

Every plant has a botanical name which is composed of two parts, the first indicating its genus and the second its species (written in italics). Species may be further divided into subspecies (subsp.). Additional names indicate whether the subject is a hybrid (a cross between different genera or species, shown by x), a cultivar (a man-made variation; the result of breeding, beginning with a capital letter in single quotes), a variety (a naturally occurring variation as opposed to a man-made one, var.) or a form (a plant with only a minor, but generally noticeable variation from the species, f.). Series or groups are collections of hybrid cultivars of like parentage. Many plants are known by two names, or have been known by another name in the past; to avoid confusion, these names may be given as synonyms (syn.). Common names (colloquial, everyday names) are also used.

THE NAMES OF CACTI AND OTHER SUCCULENTS

In the botanical world, cacti and other succulents have suffered under the successive naming regimes of 'clumpers' and 'splitters'. This means that genera have been absorbed into one another on the one hand, or divided and subdivided on the other. As a result, the botanical nomenclature is complicated, and I would ask you to bear this in mind when reading this book. On the whole, I have taken a middle road, keeping the genera in what I hope are their best-known and most easily recognized identities, and where it is helpful to the plant buyer I have retained the older form. As an example, chamaecereus or peanut cacti are very distinctive in appearance (sufficiently so to have a common name) and they include a wide range of named cultivars, so I have kept the genus name, although strictly speaking they are now listed under lobivia. By the same token, in order to save confusion, I have kept echinopsis and trichocereus separate, because one is so distinctive as a small, readily flowering genus, while the other is useful for larger, accent types of planting.

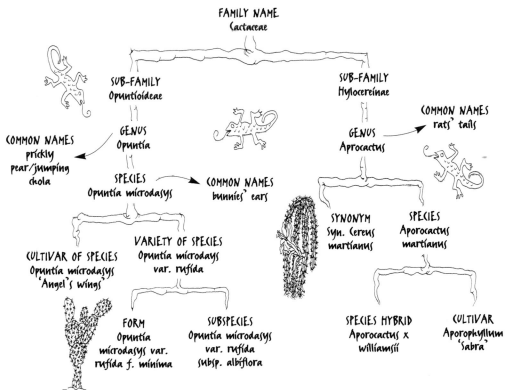

FAMILY NAME
Cactaceae

SUB-FAMILY
Opuntioideae

SUB-FAMILY
Hylocereinae

GENUS
Opuntia

GENUS
Aprocactus

COMMON NAMES
rats' tails

COMMON NAMES
prickly
pear/jumping
chola

SPECIES
Opuntia microdasys

COMMON NAMES
bunnies' ears

SYNONYM
Syn. Cereus
martianus

SPECIES
Aporocactus
martianus

VARIETY OF SPECIES
Opuntia microdays
var. rufida

CULTIVAR OF SPECIES
Opuntia microdasys
'Angel's wings'

FORM
Opuntia
microdasys var.
rufida f. minima

SUBSPECIES
Opuntia microdasys
var. rufida
subsp. albiflora

SPECIES HYBRID
Aporocactus x
williamsii

CULTIVAR
Aporophyllum
'Sabra'

KEYS

WHERE TO GROW YOUR PLANTS

All of these plants are cacti and other succulents, so they will be happy in a light, well-drained position either in the house, conservatory or glasshouse and as summer bedding in containers or in planted displays in the garden.

Those that are particularly happy or attractive as summer bedding/container plants (brought inside for the winter) are marked with **SB**.

However, some species can be grown inside but can also remain in the garden all year round in sheltered/well-drained positions, as explained in the book. These are marked with **AY**.

HEIGHT

Many subjects will remain compact in cultivation in either a pot or the ground and will not be expected to reach more than 9–12in (22–30cm) – often much smaller in cultivation. These are marked with **SML**.

Medium-height subjects growing to 12–30in (30–75cm) are marked **MED**.

Plants that reach 30in (75cm) and above are marked **TALL**.

SHAPE

The shape of the plants are indicated as follows:
Bushy/shrubby **B/S**
Columnar **CO**
Rosette forming **RF**
Succulent and fat or globular **SGL**
Creeping and mat-forming **MF**
Trailing plants **TR**
Caudiciform plants are often deciduous with a perennial rock-like engorged storage organ and vine-like spring/summer growth; these are indicated **CV**, while those without this deciduous feature are indicated **C**.
Cristate or monstrous cacti are indicated **CR/MO**. Genetic factors, damage to the growing point or maybe a virus infection are suspected to cause these interesting mutations where columnar plants grow into sculptural twisted forms and globular cacti into almost brain-like twists and folds.

ABOVE *Aeonium arboreum* contrasts with its nearly black cultivar *Aeonium arboreum* 'Zwartkop'

NAME: **AEONIUM**

Origin: Madeira, Canary Islands, Cape Verde Islands, N. Africa, Mediterranean

Description: The genus has both stemmed and stemless rosette-forming species, in various heights and often with very attractive leaf coloration.

Popular species and varieties:

SB TALL B/S *Aeonium arboreum* and its cultivars have smooth, branching stems which will form attractive candelabra if the tops are cut off (which gives you cuttings of course!) and golden-yellow flowers in late winter. *Aeonium arboreum* has bright green rosettes. *Aeonium atropurpureum* has very attractive deep maroon and green rosettes, contrasting well with the type species. *Aeonium arboreum* 'Zwartkop' is a really useful cultivar, which is far darker

than *Aeonium atropurpureum* and very impressive, with glossy black rosettes on long stems. Both of the purple aeoniums will colour up more strongly if they are given a spell outside in the summer. This also strengthens the stems. *Aeonium undulatum* has silver-grey stems with large, glossy dark green rosettes and dark yellow flowers and, like *A. arboreum*, grows up to 3ft (1m) tall.

RIGHT *Aeonium tabuliforme*

MED B/S *Aeonium domesticum* 'Variegatum' is a colourful, green and yellow, compact miniature shrub. *Aeonium haworthia* 'Variegatum' is an attractive, branching bush that grows to 24in (60cm) high, and has thin stems bearing rosettes of yellow, red and green leaves. It produces white flowers.

RF *Aeonium tabuliforme* produces bright green, flat rosettes that grow to about the size of a dinner plate.

NAME: AGAVE

Origin: The Americas and the West Indies

Description: Agaves are spiky architectural plants, with sword-like leaves growing in rosettes, excellent for summer use in containers or beds and some species can stay our all year round. They include choice variegated varieties, as well as having leaves from the longest, thinnest needle-like spikes to squat, fat short ones. They have to be huge to flower, but since this will kill the parent plant it is a marvel best not experienced. Handle them with care, because the leathery leaves often have sharp-toothed edges and ferocious terminal spines. Plant them well out of reach of children and pets, and don't put them at eye level. It's a good idea, anyway, to remove the terminal spines with scissors or secateurs if they are anywhere near through-routes, or close to where you might sit or stand. Smaller agaves are good specimen houseplants, as well as making a strong impact in the conservatory.

Popular species and varieties:

SB TALL RF *Agave americana* with its stiff, tooth-edged, blue-green leaves, and its cultivars, grow into huge rosettes, 6ft (2m) or more across. *Agave americana* 'Mediopicta' and *Agave americana* 'Mediopicta Alba' are rare and desirable, with a strong yellow or white mid-stripe on the dark green leaves, while *Agave americana* 'Variegata' has long, tapering leaves which have broad cream-yellow edges. *Agave univittata* makes offsetting

ABOVE *Agave victoriae-reginae*

ABOVE *Agave parrasana*

rosettes with glossy green leaves up to 3ft (1m) long, with darker longitudinal stripes. It has toothed leaf edges.

AY MED RF *Agave parryi* is compact with grey-blue leaves, 12in (30cm) long.

SB MED RF *Agave bracteosa* forms pale green rosettes of curved, narrow leaves, 14–20in (35–50cm) long. It has no terminal spine. *Agave filifera*, the thread agave, is very attractive, with long, tapering, rigid leaves, 30in (75cm) long which are glossy green, with white lines and long fibres splitting from the edges. *Agave parrasana* has chubby looking 24in (60cm) rosettes that are blue-grey. The leaves, which are up to 12in (30cm) long and

4–6in (10–15cm) wide, are edged with black teeth and a black terminal spine. *Agave victoriae-reginae* is a fabulous plant, 18in (46cm) tall and wide with stiff, pointed succulent leaves, forming a rosette. Its dark green leaves edged with white are so tightly interlinked, and the colours are so contrasting, that the plant almost looks artificial.

NAME: **ALOE**	RF

Origin: Africa, the Arabian peninsula, Madagascar, Cape Verde Islands
Description: Another high-impact genus, which will soon give mass to your planting ideas.

ABOVE *Aloe microstigma*

ABOVE **Aloe flowers are reminiscent of red hot pokers**

The species described below have leaves arranged in rosette form. The leaves can be triangular or long and thin, sometimes striped or spotted. In habitat they can reach 66ft (20m) in height. Their flowers are yellow, orange or red, and grow on long, arching stalks. The flowers bear a resemblance to those of red hot pokers. There are, however, smaller-growing, rosette-shaped aloes which, with their long, fleshy leaves resembling weird starfish, are also useful structural plants.

Popular species and varieties:
AY TALL *Aloe striatula* has tall dark green rosettes carried on a mass of stems and flowers freely.
AY MED *Aloe aristata* forms dense groups of up to 12 stemless rosettes of dark green, narrow leaves with very soft spines. It has branching flower stems up to 2ft (60cm) tall bearing 20 or more red or pinkish flowers, carried in late spring in Europe.
SB TALL *Aloe arborescens* has a stout, tall-growing stem with dark green fleshy rosettes of strongly toothed tapering leaves. It has tubular red flowers over 6ft (up to 2m) high. *Aloe broomii* has bright green rosettes of broad, tapering leaves with spiky edges, up to 3ft (1m) in diameter. It produces greenish yellow flowers on a long stalk. *Aloe gariepensis* has branching stems and dark green leaves with

ABOVE *Aloe gariepensis*

white spots and horny edges. It produces a tall inflorescence with yellow flowers and grows up to 3ft (1m) high like *Aloe microstigma*, which has long narrow leaves, speckled with white and with reddish teeth along the edges. It has red buds, turning into yellow flowers. *Aloe plicatilis* is one of the most distinctive of the tree aloes, with forked stems. It has fan-like clusters of strap-shaped leaves, grey-green, which are 12in (30cm) long and 1½in (4cm) wide, arranged in opposite rows. This plant bears red flowers and can reach 16ft (5m) in height. *Aloe vera* has long, tapering leaves, usually spotted white, and yellow flowers. It forms dense groups and can grow up to 6ft (2m) or so. It is thought to have all sorts of medicinal and cosmetic properties, and is a familiar ingredient of shampoos and skin creams. For all that, it has to be said, it is not one of the best-looking aloes.

SB MED *Aloe buhrii* is a stemless, rosette-forming aloe which forms multi-headed clumps with age. It is low growing, with leaves which are 16in (40cm) long and 3½in (9cm) across at the base. The leaves are yellow to grey-green with oblong or H-shaped pale markings and reddish margins. The leaf edges are smooth or slightly toothed. It has orange-red, occasionally yellow, flowers. *Aloe ciliaris* is an unusual,

rambling aloe, which makes long masses of triangular green rosettes. It can also be encouraged to climb up a trellis. *Aloe mitriformis* is another creeping aloe, with sprawling stems and thick, fleshy, blue-green leaves with small, toothed edges. *Aloe variegata*, is the partridge-breasted aloe, 12in (30cm) tall. This has thick green, triangular leaves, variegated with white. It carries red flowers on a long stem.

NAME: **ALOINOPSIS**	SML C

Origin: South Africa

Description: Aloinopsis are a group of rare, outstanding South African succulents, similar to the titanopsis, in that they also have strongly textured leaves. They grow in dense clumps and their thick, succulent leaves are carried in rosettes above their swollen caudiciform roots. They are particularly attractive if they are potted high up in the compost to expose their swollen roots, although the plants will attempt to withdraw themselves into the compost over time if you allow them to. They are good choices for flower. They like a sunny position and should not be allowed to stand around in wet compost. They are winter growers.

ABOVE *Aloinopsis luckhoffii*

Popular species and varieties: *Aloinopsis jamesii* forms an underground swollen root, bearing grey-green tapering leaves. It has golden yellow flowers with a red mid-stripe. *Aloinopsis luckhoffii* is a small, compact plant. It has thick grey-green triangular leaves with greyish tubercles and large yellow flowers.

NAME: APOROCACTUS AND APOROPHYLLUM (RATS' TAILS)   TR

Origin: The Americas
Description: Aporocacti are true species, while the aporophyllums are hybrids of aporocacti and epiphyllums. Their common name of rats'

ABOVE *Aptenia cordifolia* is an ideal plant for tall pots and hanging baskets

tails is an accurate description of the aporocacti in particular, as they have long and slender pendant stems bristling with pale spines. The aporophyllums tend to have rather fewer spines than the true species. They need a winter rest, probably because this dormant period triggers bud production. They flower dependably, and make a wonderful show with large flowers in numerous pretty shades. These plants are cacti and will flourish in a frost-free conservatory in good light. Out of flower, the long, hanging mass of trailing stems makes for a very unusual hanging-basket display.

Popular species and varieties: True species include *Aporocactus flagelliformis*, which is the true rats' tails, with deep pink to lilac flowers. It is very cold-tolerant and withstands many degrees of frost if kept dry in the winter. *Aporocactus flagriformis* is a true species with dark crimson flowers. *Aporocactus mallisonii*,

LEFT *Aporophyllum* 'Beautie'

also known as *A. flagelliformis* var. *leptophis*, has deep red flowers with a tinge of maroon in the throat. *Aporocactus martianus* has deep pink flowers that measure up to 4in (10cm) long. Plant breeders have created lots of large-flowered cultivars in a range of colours such as 'Beautie', in shades of pink, 'Brilliant', with myriads of tubular red flowers and deep orange 'Tangerine'.

ABOVE *Astrophytum ornatum*

NAME: *APTENIA CORDIFOLIA*   TR

Origin: South Africa
Description: This is a freely branching leafy succulent bearing numerous purple-red flowers. It is good for hanging baskets, trailing over the edges of shelves and benches and in urn-shaped pots with a foot.

NAME: **ASTROPHYTUM**   SML SGL

Origin: The Americas
Description: This is a very recognizable genus, which has attracted a number of common names because the speckled bodies and relative spinelessness are so very distinctive.
Popular species and varieties: *Astrophytum asterias*, or the sea urchin cactus, is a very attractive plant. Spherical and spineless, with a greyish body, patterned with white dots, It does genuinely look like the sea creature. The large yellow flowers are red-centred, making this one of the choicest members of the group. *Astrophytum capricorne*, the goat horn cactus, has a superb, white-speckled body, with a tangle of long, twisted spines. It has large yellow flowers. *Astrophytum myriostigma* is called the bishop's cap cactus, because it is completely spineless and its five angular ribs give it its suggestion of dIstinctive clerical headgear. A very attractive greyish plant, it is closely spotted with white and has large yellow flowers. *Astrophytum ornatum*, with its curved spines, body strongly speckled with white dots and light yellow flowers, is another very good-looking plant.

NAME: **CARPOBRUTUS**   AY SB MF

Origin: South Africa
Description: Evergreen mat-forming foliage choice, good for edging containers, beds, rockeries in the summer or all year round in mild areas such as southwest England.

ABOVE *Carpobrutus edulis*

111

Popular species and varieties: *Carpobrutus deliciosus* has long, greyish-green leaves on creeping stems, and pinkish-purple flowers, 3in (7–8cm) in diameter. It has edible, spherical, fig-like fruits. *Carpobrutus edulis*, the Hottentot or Kaffir fig, has creeping stems with dull green leaves, about 2½in (6cm) in length and slightly inward curving. Its flowers, which are 3in (8cm) in diameter, are yellow at first, becoming flesh coloured or pink later. Again, it bears edible, spherical fruits.

NAME: **CEPHALOCEREUS**	SB TALL CO

Origin: Mexico

Description: Although these slow-growing, columnar, bluish-green plants reach up to 50ft (15m), they rarely grow to over 3ft (1m) in height in cultivation, and flowers only appear

ABOVE **Huge white flowers will soon be opening on this** *Cereus jamacaru*

ABOVE *Cephalocereus senilis*

after many years. Spines are long, pale and woolly, and thickest at the top, especially as the plant ages, forming a cephalium, hence the common name of 'old man cactus'.

Popular species and varieties: *Cephalocereus palmeri* is noticeably hairy even when young, with brown spines and a fluffy top, eventually forming a cephalium. *Cephalocereus senilis*, one of the renowned old man cacti, is the only one sometimes known as the old man of the Andes. This is very showy, with masses of long and tangled white hair. It is, unfortunately, rather slow-growing, but since it seems to like a more restricted root run and a free-draining compost, it is well worth underpotting.

NAME: CEREUS   SB TALL CO

Origin: South America

Description: Tall and narrow bluish green columns with angled spiny stems.

Popular species and varieties: *Cereus aethiops*, growing to almost 5–6ft (2m) in height, is a worthwhile choice. Its flowers, which are white, sometimes flushed pink, are produced at an earlier stage than most cereus. *Cereus grandicostatus* is an eye-catchingly azure blue when young, eventually becoming more yellow green. The tall columns produce huge 10in (25cm) white flowers. *Cereus jamacaru* has attractive bluish green ribbed columns. It bears very large white flowers up to 3ft (1m) or so tall. *Cereus peruvianus* produces tall-growing blue-green columns with six to eight ribs and large white flowers on old specimens. *Cereus peruvianus* x *azureus* is a vigorous hybrid of two tall-growing blue-green-stemmed columnar plants, so it is worth growing if you want quick in-filling. This species has huge white flowers. *Cereus stenogonus* has branching, bluish green columns with four or five ribs. It will eventually produce large pink flowers. This is such a vigorous grower that it is an excellent candidate for grafting purposes. Grows up to 28in (70cm) tall. *Cereus validus* is another quick-growing species, with bluish green ribbed columns and large white to reddish flowers. Grows up to 6ft (2m) high.

CR/MO *Cereus jamacaru* var. *monstrosus* is a fabulous, glossy green monster. *Cereus peruvianus* var. *monstrosus* is a glossy blue-green sculptured work of art.

NAME: CEROPEGIA   TR

Origin: South Africa

Description: These are very useful plants. They have delicate foliage, often a lilac-grey colour, which is especially attractive and makes a good contrast to both green and purple-toned

ABOVE *Ceropegia woodii 'Variegata'*

plants. This is a genus which enjoys a slightly more shaded location.

Popular species and varieties: *Ceropegia linearis* subsp. *woodii*, syn *C. woodii* is the species you are most likely to meet. Its attractive grey heart-shaped leaves have purple markings, and it bears small purple lantern-shaped flowers which appear very delicate and exotic. *Ceropegia woodii* 'Variegata' is another excellent choice with its white-splashed leaves.

NAME: *CHAMAECEREUS* SYN *ECHINOPSIS CHAMAECEREUS*   AY SB SML SGL

Origin: South America

Description: Chamaecereus (also known as chamaelobivia) are known too as peanut cacti because of their segmented habit. It is common now to regard the chamaecereus genus as

ABOVE **An unnamed hybrid of** *Chamacereus silvestrii*

absorbed into lobivia, but I am treating them separately here because the hybrids are so distinctive in their own right.

Popular species and varieties: The species is *Chamaecereus silvestrii*, which has a pale green body, forming finger-like clumps and carrying large scarlet flowers. It is a sturdy grower. However, plant breeders have also concentrated on this genus to produce a number of attractive large-flowered hybrids with a choice of white, yellow and orange flowers. **CR/MO** is the 'deformed' version, with thickened stems ending in a flattened, club-like cristate head. It has scarlet flowers like the species. *Chamaecereus silvestrii* 'Andy' is a robust columnar plant with attractive gold flowers. *Chamaecereus silvestrii* 'Ragged Robin' is particularly worth seeking out. As the name suggests, its purple-red flowers have 'ragged' petals like the wild flower of the same name. *C. silvestrii* 'Yellow Bird' is an unusual yellow-flowered hybrid. You will also come across numerous unnamed cultivars, including at least one white-flowered form and a pretty lilac one.

NAME: **CLEISTOCACTUS**	SB TALL CO

Origin: South America

Description: These columnar branching cacti have pale needle-like spines.

Popular species and varieties: *Cleistocactus buchtienii* is a useful fast-growing, columnar cactus, forming clusters of tall stems with reddish brown spines. It has wine-red tubular flowers, over 2in (5cm) long. *Cleistocactus jujuyensis* forms beautiful cream-spined columns with long tubular flowers in an unusual bluish carmine. *Cleistocactus straussii*, the silver torch cactus, is a fabulous plant, with tall white columns covered in beautiful soft white spines. With time it will make slender and stately clumps. It has long but rudimentary scarlet flowers.

LEFT *Cleistocactus straussii*

ABOVE *Conophytum subfenestratum*

NAME: **CONOPHYTUM** SML SGL

Origin: South Africa

Description: These are popular clumping plants, many of which resemble living stones (lithops). They, too, are autumn flowering.

Popular species and varieties: *Conophytum pearsonii* is bluish with mauve-pink flowers. *Conophytum subfenestratum* is a clump-forming species. It has a cylindrical body 1in (2.5cm) long, which is pale green with darker green spots and bears white to lilac-pink flowers. *Conophytum ursprungianum* is an extremely beautiful species with light green heads covered in dark green dots and has white flowers. *Conphytum verrucosum* is a stone-like species, having brown stems with many grey dots.

NAME: **COPIAPOA** SML SGL

Origin: South America

Description: These plants deserve a place in this directory on the strength of their colour alone, which makes them one of the most interesting groups of spherical cacti. They vary from floury white through grey-green to dark brown/black, and most species have perfumed yellow flowers.

RIGHT *Copiapoa humilis*

Popular species and varieties: *Copiapoa humilis* is small, spherical and deep green to olive green, sometimes with a reddish overlay, and bristly with fine white spines and a longer central spine, and bearing yellow flowers. *Copiapoa hypogaea* is a fabulous, very dramatic black plant with black spines and contrasting yellow flowers tinged with pink. *Copiapoa tenuissima* is a striking olive green, with grey spines and yellowish pink flowers.

NAME: **COTYLEDON** SB MED–TALL B/S

Origin: South Africa

Description: Grey green succulent leaves.

Popular species and varieties:

TALL *Cotyledon wallichii* has thick, branching stems covered with the stumps of old leaves, attractive, peeling bark and grey-green, long, narrow, succulent leaves and yellow flowers. Grows to over 6ft (2m) tall, but is slow growing.

LEFT *Cotyledon orbiculata*

MED *Cotyledon orbiculata* has a superb grey bloom on the leaves and carries red and yellow flowers on a long stalk. *Cotyledon undulata* (syn. *Cotyledon orbiculata* var. *oblonga*) has thick leaves covered in a grey bloom and, as the Latin suggests, the leaves have distinctly wavy edges, sometimes with a red tinge. This plant produces orange-red flowers on a long stalk.

NAME: **CRASSULA**

Origin: South Africa mainly, but also some parts of Madagascar and Asia

Description: This useful genus offers an unbeatable range of species, which are almost infinitely variable. They are trouble-free plants, which grow vigorously, and will tolerate any position from sunny to shaded, with consequent

ABOVE *Crassula ovata* 'Pink Beauty'

ABOVE During winter, *Crassula* 'Silver Springtime' produces attractive pink flowers that make a lovely display

ABOVE Well-tended crassulas, like this *Crassula ovata*, will often reward you with a mass of tiny white flowers in winter

alterations to the size and colour of their foliage. As houseplants they are useful for winter flowers and for their choice of shape and leaf colour, and some make attractive mock 'bonsai' specimens. A number of them are useful for containers and for summer bedding. They are very easy to propagate from cuttings. There is a whole host to choose from but some of the best are listed below.

Popular species and varieties:

MF The mat-forming crassulas can be used in pots on shelving, where they soften the otherwise stark geometry of the display stand. They are also good in cascade pots where they can be used to spill over the edges. In beds in the conservatory they will give you rapid ground cover, and they will also work as underplanting in mixed pots and containers. *Crassula lanuginosa* is a typical mat-forming species, with grey, pointed leaves which are softly hairy. It has small, white flowers. *Crassula pellucida* subsp. *marginalis* is a really versatile choice, which will colour up into a

spectacular maroon in the sunniest spot. Its leaves, which will become compressed and fatter, are bi-coloured maroon and green in slightly shaded conditions, becoming a rich, dark green in deeper shade. In all of its metamorphoses it will produce a mass of white flowers in the winter months.

SML–MED B/S These species are attractive and varied plants, grown for their colourful foliage effects, interesting forms and leaf shapes. *Crassula columnella* grows, as the name suggests, in strange, compressed columns of green to yellow-green leaves which develop a red tint in strong sunlight. It reaches 6in (15cm) in height, with stems which are 3–4in (8–10cm) tall, and it bears greenish white flowers. *Crassula falcata* is worth growing for

117

ABOVE *Crassula sarcocaulis*

its spirals of blue-grey bloomed, succulent leaves, as well as for its masses of red flowers. *Crassula obliqua* 'Variegata' has very showy grass-green leaves, strongly marked with lemon and cream. *Crassula obliqua* var. *gollum*, is an unusual plant, with the leaves folded and united into solid tapering cylinders. A must!

Good for winter flower *Crassula cooperi* is a fine miniature, flowering profusely in winter. *Crassula lactea* is a useful bushy species, growing up to 16in (40cm) high, with large thick leaves. This plant is particularly noted for its mass of white flowers produced in winter or early spring. *Crassula* 'Silver Springtime' is especially attractive for its pyramidal rosettes of compact, very thick leaves with minute grey hairs, as well as for its white flowers. *Crassula* 'Starburst' is a fascinating little plant. It forms small columns with triangular leaves, carrying clusters of pure white flowers in the winter. *Crassula* 'Morgan's Beauty' is a compact,

highly succulent, grey-leaved cultivar with red flowers. *Crassula tomentosa* grows up to 24in (60cm) tall. It has densely hairy, grey-green leaves arranged in loose rosettes and small, pale yellow flowers.

Good for the garden SB TALL B/S *Crassula ovata*, or the money plant, is confusingly also known as *C. argentea* and *C. portulacea*, and it will be found under all three names. The species and its cultivars make wonderful mass plantings in a bed or large container, where the foliage contrast looks very fine. It has a thick trunk and many branches, with glossy, coin-shaped leaves and small white flowers in the winter. It can reach over 6ft (2m) in height. *Crassula ovata* 'Blue Bird' is a pretty cultivar which has grey-green leaves. *Crassula ovata* 'Hummel's Sunset' is a very colourful cultivar, with heavily variegated yellow, red and green leaves, especially when grown in strong light. For faux bonsai, in time it will grow into a very convincing larger tree, up to 3ft (1m) or more tall. It has a distinctive ringed trunk, branches clothed with succulent leaves and a mass of starry flowers in the winter.

AY MED B/S *Crassula sarcocaulis* has narrow, dark green leaves and lots of pink flowers, produced in summer. Grows into an attractive miniature tree up to 2ft (60cm) high and 1½ft (45cm) across. Very frost resistant. *Crassula sarcocaulis* subsp. *rupicola* has white flowers. Also a good houseplant potted up as a 'bonsai' specimen.

NAME: *CYPHOSTEMMA JUTTAE*	TALL C

Origin: South Africa
Description: This can eventually reach 6ft (2m) in height. It has a correspondingly huge caudex, an attractively peeling papery covering to its yellow bark, and thick branches which carry oval green leaves 8 x 2½in (20 x 6cm).

NAME: **DELOSPERMA**	AY MF

Origin: South Africa
Description: A spreading succulent with fleshy leaves which may die back in a cold winter but will reappear every spring to clothe pond edges and rockeries, also good for edging containers.

ABOVE *Delosperma cooperi* is a hardy succulent which has carpets of lilac flowers all summer

ABOVE *Cyphostemma juttae* is shown here with its eye-catching, swollen caudex

Popular species and varieties: *Delosperma cooperi* has dark green leaves and carries a mass of lilac flowers from mid- to late spring to the first frost. *D. nubigenum* has bright green leaves and carries abundant, beautiful bright yellow daisy-like flowers making a dazzling carpet – but only in the spring. Grows to 1in (2.5cm) or so high with an indefinite spread.

NAME: **ECHEVERIA**	SB MED RF

Origin: The Americas
Description: These are some of the best foliage plants you can possibly have, both for the house and conservatory and for summer bedding. Many beautiful cultivars have been developed, and their rosettes come in a range of pastel shades, pinks, turquoises and lilacs, through really dark maroons to almost black.

ABOVE *Echeveria glauca*

ABOVE *Echeveria 'Harry Butterfield'*

ABOVE *Echeveria 'Red Edge'*

ABOVE *Echeveria 'Easter Bonnet'*

Planted up together they make fabulous contrasting arrangements. They can also be used to set off taller accent plants if used as a colourful underplanting in a container, and they are really pretty planted up en masse in a container full of a single cultivar. Their long-lasting cymes of flowers are pink or yellow and much loved by flower arrangers. There are a multitude to choose from but some of the best are listed below.

Popular species and varieties: *Echeveria affinis* has impressive dark olive green rosettes, almost black. *Echeveria* 'Afterglow' has impressive large, deep red-to-purple rosettes. *Echeveria albicans* has powdery grey-blue leaves, forming an attractive rosette. *Echeveria* 'Blue Curls' has a rosette of wavy blue-green leaves. *Echeveria* 'Black Prince', like all the dark echeverias, is highly prized. It has red-maroon to almost black leaves. *Echeveria dereceana* has beautiful rosettes of pointed grey or grey-brown leaves. *Echeveria elegans* is a branching species with an intense grey bloom. *Echeveria* 'Easter Bonnet' has really attractive rosettes of grey, blue-green leaves with crinkled edges. *Echeveria* *glauca* has grey-bloomed leaves in large, clustering, rosettes. *Echeveria* 'Harry Butterfield' has dramatically coloured round green leaves with bright red edges. The leaf edges are slightly wavy, the rosettes medium sized. *Echeveria lindsayana* has striking rosettes of pointed blue-grey leaves, tipped with red. *Echeveria* 'Mauna Loa' (named after a Hawaiian volcano) is multicoloured bronze and olive green. *Echeveria meridian* has vigorous, bright green rosettes which reach 12in (30cm) across. *Echeveria nodulosa* 'Painted Beauty' is a striking cultivar. Its green leaves have strongly contrasting red and brown streaks and patches all over them. *Echeveria* 'Painted Frills' has rosettes of wavy red, brown and olive-green leaves. *Echeveria* 'Perle von Nurnberg' is an amazing pale lilac cultivar. *Echeveria* 'Rondellii' has blue-green rosettes of tapering, bristly leaves. *Echeveria* 'Red Edge' develops large rosettes of rounded to slightly wavy leaves. Green, and marked with red lines and patches, these have bright red edges. The flower spike is very stout.

Echeveria runyonii 'Topsy-turvy' offsets freely to form clumps of long grey leaves, widening at the tips and with the leaf sides curling inwards. *Echeveria setosa* is a very unusual plant and one of the best echeverias, with attractive green-grey leaves covered with dense white hairs. *Echeveria subrigida* has large, very pretty, grey-blue rosettes which reach up to 2ft (60cm) across. *Echeveria subsessilis* has rosettes of blue-grey leaves with red edges.

NAME: ECHINOCACTUS   SB MED SGL

Origin: The Americas

Description: These are fat, globular cacti, which are covered in stout yellow spines. They become very large with age, almost like big fat pumpkins. They reach 3 x 3ft (1 x 1m) in height and diameter in habitat, but much less in cultivation. There is also a white-spined form.

Popular species and varieties: *Echinocactus grusonii*, the golden barrel cactus or, less kindly, mother-in-law's chair or cushion.

ABOVE *Echinocactus grusonii*

ABOVE *Echinocereus reichenbachii var. baileyi*

ABOVE *Echinocereus pentalophus*

NAME: **ECHINOCEREUS**	AY SB SML SGL

Origin: The Americas

Description: Echinocereus is a large-flowered genus of more than 70 species of showy plants, many with attractive spines, which bear colourful flowers up to 5in (12cm) across. These plants can give diversity to a collection because they grow in a variety of shapes, and they can be globular, columnar or trailing. Their flowers come mainly in shades of yellow, orange, pink and purple and have the advantage that they are frequently long lived.

Popular species and varieties: These choices will grow outside all year round in a sheltered and well-drained postion, otherwise use for summer planting. *Echinocereus pentalophus* has long, thick stems, which are pale green and have a sprawling habit. The flowers are very showy, growing up to 5in (12cm) long, and are coloured lilac or pink with a white throat. *Echinocereus reichenbachii* var. *baileyi* has attractive white spines, which are tinged pink, and large, light purple flowers. *Echinocereus triglochidiatus* has sparse, but long, white and black spines and long-lasting deep red flowers. *Echinocereus viridiflorus* is a freely offsetting species, with unusual and attractive yellowish green flowers.

NAME: **ECHINOFOSSULOCACTUS**	MED SGL

Origin: South America

Description: This genus (which is also known as stenocactus) has an interesting, much-crinkled and wavy, ribbed habit, appearing almost artificially pleated, often with very strong spination.

Popular species and varieties:
Echinofossulocactus crispatus grows quite quickly for this genus; it has numerous, narrow, wavy ribs and purple flowers.
Echinofossulocactus heteracanthus is strikingly corrugated, as it has 40 to 50 thin, wavy, closely pleated ribs. It bears greenish yellow

ABOVE *Echinofossulocatus crispatus*

ABOVE **Echinopsis species**

flowers. *Echinofossulocactus tricuspidatus* has up to 55 wavy ribs and yellow-green flowers.

NAME: ECHINOPSIS   SML SGL

Origin: South America
Description: These are easily grown plants, often clustering with age. Most species have spectacular and very large tubular flowers, which are often perfumed and open at night.
Popular species and varieties: *Echinopsis* 'Green Gold' has pale yellow perfumed flowers, usually opening in the evening. *Echinopsis eyriesii* is a reliable bloomer, with huge white flowers up to 10in (25cm) long. *Echinopsis* 'Gerrits Lemon' has pretty, pale yellow flowers. *Echinopsis* 'Haku Jo' is a cultivar of Japanese origin, which has an attractive blue-green body with amazing felted ribs. It bears large, white, strongly perfumed flowers with narrow, curving petals. *Echinopsis silvestrii* readily produces incredible, 8in (20cm) long, pure white flowers. Has to be seen to be believed! Like the chamaecereus, the echinopsis have attracted the attention of plant breeders, so it is worth seeking out the 'Paramount hybrids' which have been bred for their huge, brightly coloured flowers.

NAME: EPIPHYLLUM HYBRIDS
(ORCHID CACTI)   TR

Origin: South America, West Indies
Description: Although they are cacti, the layman would not recognize them as such. Their long, pale strap-like 'leaves' are actually stems, and they have residual areoles with spines erupting from them. They are useful foliage in-fillers, either suspended from hanging baskets or wall containers, or tied to trellis, canes or other plant supports, but even devotees would hesitate to call them beautiful

123

ABOVE **Orchid cactus**

until they flower. They produce massive, sometimes highly scented blooms that are reminiscent of the cup-shaped blooms you find on water lilies. They have been bred purely for the size and colour of their flowers, which are available in a wide range of shades. There is, however, no blue, which means that 'purple' has to be interpreted fairly loosely as a deep reddish hue – like the lilac red of the ubiquitous Christmas cactus.

Popular species and varieties: True species that have been used in hybridization include *Epiphyllum crenatum*, with white, slightly fragrant flowers, *E. oxypetalum*, a large, fragrant, white, night-bloomer and 'Deutsche Kaiserine', actually *Nopalxochia phyllanthoides*, which has beautiful shell-pink flowers and a mass of small blooms. The cultivars are available in a huge range of colours and sizes, but look out for 'Dante', with beautiful wide-open flowers, with lavender-pink inner petals with purple mid-stripe and purple outer petals, tinged with orange and red. Strongly perfumed 'Jenkinsonii' has large, easily produced flowers in scarlet with orange-red mid-stripe and violet in the throat. 'Pride of Bell'

has large flowers with long thin sepals, white with rose and orchid striping the petals and most of the sepals. 'Denis Kucera' has flat open petals of orange and violet and extra-large flowers. 'Cooperi' is an old favourite with highly scented white flowers with yellow outer petals. 'Dobson's Yellow' is free flowering with creamy yellow blooms and 'Reward' has rich, soft yellow, wide-open large flowers.

NAME: **EUPHORBIA**

Origin: South Africa

Description: Euphorbia is a massive genus, which includes many traditional garden shrubs, but in this context its interest as a genus lies in its demonstration of parallel evolution in Africa instead of the Americas. The African euphorbias are globular and columnar cactus-like plants which have thorns, instead of spines growing from areoles, and often have tiny, rudimentary

ABOVE **As its name suggests,** *Euphorbia candelabrum* var. *erythrae* **is a many-branched plant**

leaves. All euphorbias have a milky, irritant sap, so take care to handle them with gloves if they are damaged in any way and oozing.

Popular species and varieties:

SB TALL CO & B/S These magnificent, tall-branched specimens, which are remarkably cactus-like in appearance, will grow into 6ft (2m) specimens much more quickly than the true cacti. *Euphorbia candelabrum* var. *erythraea* has dark green stems with a lighter green central band. It forms branches like a candelabrum with small leaves, and is very architectural. *Euphorbia canariensis* has stout, branching columns, four- or five-angled, with flat sides between. It can eventually reach several feet (metres) in height. *Euphorbia coerulescens* is a blue-grey branched shrub with ½in (1.5cm) long spines and a yellow inflorescence reaching 5ft (1.5m) tall. *Euphorbia mauritanica* is the milk tree of the

ABOVE *Euphorbia milii 'Thira'*

Boers – but please don't drink it! The common name refers to the extremely irritant milky sap it exudes when damaged. It is a thornless shrub, which branches from the base, and grows up

ABOVE *Euphorbia resinifera* grows in large and thick-stemmed clumps

to 5ft (1.5m) tall. *Euphorbia resinifera* is a very thick-stemmed species, soon forming giant clumps. It displays yellow flowers.

MED B/S *Euphorbia milii*, the crown of thorns, is a useful houseplant as it is an interesting thorny euphorbia which makes a glorious show of 'flower' when its bracts, which can be red or yellow, and makes a mass display on the plant.

SM SGL *Euphorbia obesa* is almost freakishly spherical and spineless, and develops strongly marked grey, green and red stripes with age. The patterning is so strong that it can almost appear like tartan. This species has insignificant yellow flowers.

RIGHT *Faucaria tigrina*

ABOVE *Euphorbia milii*

NAME: **FAUCARIA**	SML SGL

Origin: South Africa

Description: Faucaria are all interesting miniature succulent plants, with markedly toothed leaf edges which look like the mouths of ferocious, if tiny, green animals! They have the bonus of producing large, golden yellow flowers.

Popular species and varieties: *Faucaria candida* has large white flowers, very unusual for this genus, while *Faucaria longifolia* has long, narrow, grey-green leaves and large, dark yellow flowers. *Faucaria tigrina* is the eponymous tiger's jaws, with yellow flowers. *Faucaria tuberculosa* has thick triangular-shaped leaves with tubercles and teeth, and the usual large yellow flowers.

NAME: **FEROCACTUS**	MED–TALL SGL

Origin: The Americas

Description: Ferocactus is a heavily spined genus, with a distinctive, large, fat, globular form which has given its members the common name of barrel cacti.

Popular species and varieties: *Ferocactus glaucescens* is a bluish green spherical plant which produces yellow flowers when quite young – an unusual feature for a ferocactus.

ABOVE *Ferocactus peninsulae*

Ferocactus peninsulae is a very heavily spined barrel cactus. *Ferocactus peninsulae* var. *townsendianus* has a shortly cylindrical-shaped body with attractive ribs, often spiralled or wavy. The flowers are pink in the middle with a greenish yellow border.

NAME: **FRITHIA**   SML SGL

Origin: South Africa
Description: These are choice, stemless plants that are very tiny and clustering, with distinct

windows at the end of each leaf.
Popular species and varieties: *Frithia pulchra* is a windowed, clump-forming mesembryanthemum. It produces flowers of various colours, although most frequently purple with a white centre. *Frithia pulchra* var. *minor* is an unusual white-flowered form.

NAME: **FURCRAEA SELLOA VAR. MARGINATA**   SB RF TALL

Origin: South America
Description: A solitary trunk topped with a stiff rosette of sword-like leaves, green with yellow margins, reaching 5ft (1.5m) tall.

NAME: **GYMNOCALYCIUM**   SML SGL

Origin: South America
Description: This is an excellent group for the beginner or advanced collector because it offers such a wide variety of form, spination, flower and colour. There are more than 60 species in all, and those listed below are some of the prettiest for flower.
Popular species and varieties:
Gymnocalycium baldianum is a dark grey to bluish green plant bearing magnificent flowers in shades of red and maroon. It is one of the

ABOVE *Frithia pulchra*

ABOVE *Furcraea selloa var. marginata*

127

ABOVE *Gymnocalycium baldianum*

best gymnocalyciums. *Gymnocalycium damsii* is deep green, often tinged red or brown, with large pink flowers. *Gymnocalycium multiflorum* is a bright green plant, eventually clumping, with flattened, curved, yellow spines. It has pretty bell-shaped pink flowers shading to almost white. *Gymnocalycium platense* and *G. quehlianum* both have strikingly attractive white flowers with contrasting red throats. *Gymnocalycium stellatum* has an unusual olive-green to grey-green body which has brown or black spines and carries large, pure white flowers.

NAME: **HOYA**	TR

Origin: Asia, Australia and the Pacific Islands
Description: These are fabulous evergreen climbing and/or trailing plants, which are grown for their exotic waxy flowers and dark-green glossy foliage. They make wonderful conservatory and indoor subjects in a slightly shaded position, so make sure you give them some shade in the summer months. Apart from *Hoya carnosa* and *H. kuhlii*, they need to be kept warmer than most of the other succulents

– around 10°F (50°C) upwards – which means that they will not flourish in a conservatory which is only kept frost-free. They like a rich, well-drained soil, with moderate watering in full growth; water sparingly otherwise.
Popular species and varieties: *Hoya carnosa* is the best-known and the most widely available of the hoyas, with climbing stems and thick, succulent leaves. It bears amazing pale pink flowers in clusters. The waxy texture and intricate detail of the flower heads make them appear almost artificial, especially as the flowers are so long-lasting. Along with *H. kuhlii*, it is the most cool-tolerant of the hoyas. *Hoya bilobata* is particularly useful as it produces umbels of small red flowers all year round. *Hoya kuhlii* is mainly a trailing plant, but it will also climb. Its flowers are pink with a red centre. *Hoya linearis* produces wonderful cascades of narrow leaves and pendant, waxy white flowers. Like *H. carnosa* and *H. kuhlii* it is more cool tolerant than most hoyas.

NAME: **IPOMOEA**	TALL CV

Origin: South America and South Africa
Description: Some species have an underground reservoir from which they

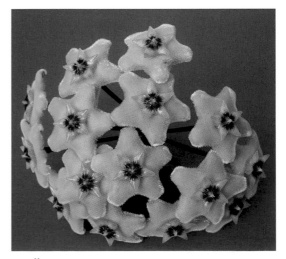

ABOVE *Hoya carnosa*

ABOVE *Ipomoea holubii*

ABOVE *Kalanchoe 'Mirabella'*

regenerate each year, while others have greatly swollen stems. They are all rare and considered desirable.

Popular species and varieties: *Ipomoea carnea*, from South America, has tall stems, initially pear-shaped and becoming more slender towards the leafy top. *Ipomoea holubii*, from South Africa, has a caudex to 8in (20cm) in diameter, with thin stems produced from the top, and large deep pink to purple flowers.

NAME: KALANCHOE

Origin: Madagascar,

Description: These kalanchoes are nothing like the mass-produced, almost perpetually flowering pot plants found in supermarkets all year round. Kalanchoes appear in many shapes and sizes, including the following useful shrubs with attractive foliage colour.

Popular species and varieties:

MED B/S *Kalanchoe daigremontiana*, or mother of thousands, has tall stems with triangular grey-olive leaves which develop miniature replica plants from their edges. These drop off and form little colonies. Children love them. *Kalanchoe fedtschenkoi* grows into a small bush with blue-green leaves with brown margins, and brownish pink flowers. *Kalanchoe fedtschenkoi* 'Variegata' is a really

colourful species, which has beautiful blue-grey leaves with yellow and cream markings edged with red. *Kalanchoe pumila* is an upright species which has attractive leaves with a soft grey bloom and pretty lilac flowers. In time the weight will make it droop down, when it can be used in the same way as the trailing kalanchoes below. *Kalanchoe tomentosa* is a

ABOVE *Kalanchoe pumila*

much sought-after beauty with grey, furry leaves patterned with brown and yellow markings. Other kalanchoes include these loosely trailing, leafy plants with pretty and profuse flowers. **MED TR** *Kalanchoe manginii* is a superb trailing plant with narrow stems and pendant bell-shaped red flowers. *Kalanchoe* 'Mirabella' has flowers with approximately ¾in (2cm) long, red petals and a yellow tube. *Kalanchoe* 'Wendy' is a lovely plant, ideal for hanging baskets. It is semi-erect with glossy green leaves, and bears long-lasting ¾in (2cm) long, bell-shaped, pinkish red flowers with yellow tips in late winter.

NAME: *KLEINIA REPENS* SYN.
**   *SENECIO SERPENS***   SB MED B/S

Origin: South Africa
Description: This is another really useful succulent, with a mass of beautiful blue leaves and yellow flowers. It produces a clutch of thin fingers, which makes it a good plant for hanging or edging.

ABOVE **A bed of lampranthus cultivars**

NAME: LAMPRANTHUS   AY SB MF

Origin: South Africa
Description: These mat-forming succulents have originated in semi-desert areas. They have narrow, succulent leaves and are grown for their colourful, daisy-like flowers which are borne in profusion throughout summer.
Popular species and varieties: *Lampranthus aurantiacus* has orange flowers and grey-green leaves. *Lampranthus roseus* syn. *Mesembryanthemum multiradiatum* is a low-growing mesembryanthemum which has clumping grey-green leaves and very pretty purple flowers carried all summer. *Lampranthus spectabilis* is a variable succulent with purple flowers, sometimes white, and mid-green leaves. There are also lots of cultivars in various colours, like apricot, pink, red, yellow, etc. They like poor soil in a sunny, well-drained site. The plants can survive in mild areas (treat as half-hardy elsewhere) and *L. spectabilis* has naturalized in southwest England.

ABOVE **Kleinia repens**

ABOVE **Lithops**

NAME: **LITHOPS**   SML SGL

Origin: South Africa

Description: These are the definitive living stones, which are found growing half-submerged in very dry areas of southern Africa. They have a pair of very succulent leaves, and the plant bodies strongly resemble spotted and mottled pebbles, hence their popular name. They grow by shedding their skin like a snake, with a newer, fatter and freshly invigorated plant emerging from the remnants of the dried skin of the first version. With age they form fine, many-headed clusters. Their large, daisy-like flowers, which appear from the fissured centre of the plant, are often produced when the plants are quite small. They produce their white or yellow flowers in the autumn.

Popular species and varieties: *Lithops bromfieldii* var. *insularis* 'Sulphurea' is worth hunting out, because it is a very unusual brightly coloured lime-green plant with darker green mottling, lines or patches. It has yellow flowers. *Lithops lesliei* is greyish yellow to coffee, with greenish brown spots and furrows; its flowers are golden yellow, very occasionally

white. *Lithops lesliei* 'Albinica' has a distinctly translucent, grass-green body, with a yellowish sheen and a yellow patterning. *Lithops localis* forms clumps of pinkish grey heads with dark green dots and approximately 1in (2.5cm) diameter flowers. *Lithops optica* 'Rubra', is the choicest of the lithops. It is a highly unusual, brightly coloured, mat-forming crimson plant with brown-green patches or lines. The flowers are white and pink. *Lithops salicola* is grey with dotted darker grey windows and white flowers. *Lithops schwantesii* is dark grey to orange, with bluish marks and white flowers.

NAME: **LOBIVIA**   SML SGL

Origin: South America (actually Bolivia – the name is an anagram!)

Description: Easy to grow, these compact globular plants have large flowers in dazzling reds, yellows, pinks and white – often in strongly contrasting colours with darker centres.

Popular species and varieties: *Lobivia arachnacantha* is a small clumping plant with huge glossy purple flowers that are often bigger than the plant itself. *Lobivia aurea* is a white-spined plant with attractive, two-toned, lemon yellow flowers with deep yellow centres.

ABOVE ***Lobivia pentlandii***

Lobivia aurea var. *dobeana* is a clumping species. Its amazing red flowers have contrasting bright yellow centres. *Lobivia chrysantha* subsp. *jajoiana* has elongating plant bodies and it is probably the best species for really flashy flowers, as it has readily produced beaker-shaped wine red or pink flowers with dramatic black centres. *Lobivia haematantha* var. *amblayensis* is only around 1in (2.5cm) high and wide, although it is often clumping in cultivation. It has large flowers 2½–4in (6–10cm) across in yellow or orange. *Lobivia pentlandii* is a dark, grey-green plant with large flowers which come in an astonishing range of colours – yellow, orange, pink, violet or red.

NAME: **MAMMILLARIA**	SML SGL

Origin: The Americas

Description: The genus mammillaria contains over 300 species and is the most popular of all groups of cacti and the most popular choice for a specialist collection. Some of the species are excellent for flowers which are produced in the form of a ring around the top of the plant and are succeeded by fleshy red seed pods, giving the plant an interesting appearance

ABOVE *Mammillaria bombycina*

throughout the winter, while other mammillaria species are really good plants for interesting and attractive spines, rather than, or as well as, for their flowers.

Popular species and varieties:

For flowers *Mammillaria boolii* is a choice species covered in glassy white spines, some of them hooked. It also bears large orange flowers. *Mammillaria fraileana* is a cylindrical plant with white flowers which are flushed pink and are produced in a ring near the crown of the plant. *Mammillaria glassii* var. *ascensionis* has many advantages: it is a rapidly clumping species, covered in attractive, fluffy white spines, and is one of the earliest to bloom. The flowers are an attractive pink. *Mammillaria laui* has yellow spines and magenta flowers. *Mamillaria laui* f. *subducta* is densely covered in cream or white spines and has deep pink flowers. *Mammillaria longiflora* is notable for its large white and pink flowers. *Mammillaria longimamma* has long, bright green tubercles and large yellow flowers, readily produced in the early spring. *Mammillaria zeilmanniana* is one of the best mammillarias for a long and showy display of flowers. This superb freely

ABOVE *Mammillaria boolii*

ABOVE *Mammillaria bocasana*

flowering species has rings of lilac flowers and makes a fabulous show. *Mammillaria zeilmanniana* var. *alba* is like its parent, but with rings of white flowers. Mix them together for an eye-watering display.

For spines *Mammillaria albicans* is a cylindrical plant covered in showy, pure white spines. It has large white flowers with a pale pink mid-stripe and grows up to 8in (20cm) high. *Mammillaria angelensis* has fabulous white spines and large, bell-shaped white flowers. *Mammillaria bocasana* is a clustering cream-flowered species with masses of white wool and white spines. *Mammillaria bombycina* has very attractive spines, and soon makes imposing clumps. *Mammillaria decipiens* var. *camptotricha* is also known as the bird's nest cactus. It has very long, showy, curved and interlacing soft spines and white flowers. *Mammillaria hahniana* is a desirable species with long white hairs and purple flowers. *Mammillaria lanata* (also known as M. *supertexta*) is a lovely plant covered in short white spines. It has small reddish flowers, immersed in a mass of long white wool. *Mammillaria lenta* is a magnificent tight white-

spined species, with white flowers, and is known as the snowball cactus. *Mammillaria pennispinosa* is a delightful species, immediately recognizable by its beautiful white, feathery spines. *Mammillaria prolifera* develops into fluffy cream mounds, rapidly clustering. *Mammillaria senilis* is one of the most beautiful of all cacti. The fluffy white plants are completely covered in silvery white spines, and mature plants cluster. It also has large red flowers. *Mammillaria spinosissima* 'Pico' is an attractive cultivar with very long, fine white spines and deep pink flowers.

CR/MO SML These densely spined waves of undulating yellow or white plant are stupendous, like convoluted spiny brains. *Mammillaria elongata* var. *cristata* is a beautiful cristate form of the golden-spined species. *Mammillaria lanata* var. *cristata* forms twisting waves covered in short white spines and bearing red flowers. *Mammillaria zeilmanniana* var. *cristata* is a rare cristate form of this popular species. It grows in curving waves rather than in the usual globular form.

ABOVE *Mammillaria zeilmanniana*

ABOVE *Neoporteria subgibbosa*

ABOVE *Notocactus schlosseri*

NAME: **NEOPORTERIA**   SML SGL

Origin: South America
Description: These have interesting bodies which are often coloured red-brown, olive-green and other unusual tones, with interesting spination. They usually have pretty pink flowers, which appear almost throughout the year (in the late autumn and the early spring, as well as in the early summer) so they are useful for extra flower.
Popular species and varities: *Neoporteria subgibbosa* is grey-spined with pretty pink and white flowers. *Neoporteria villosa* grows into a striking dark green, almost black, plant with grey spines and magenta flowers.

NAME: **NOTOCACTUS**   SML SGL

Origin: South America
Description: Notocactus is a deservedly popular genus of globular or short columnar plants with a range of spination. Their showy flowers, which are usually bright yellow, are reliably produced.
Popular species and varieties: *Notocactus buiningii* is attractive even when not in flower because of its light, grass-green colour, symmetrical ribs and spination. It also has very large, yellow flowers. *Notocactus graessneri* is a popular, yellow-spined, yellow-flowered species. *Notocactus haselbergii* is a lovely, small-growing species, which is entirely covered with soft white to yellow spines. It has long-lasting, unusual fiery red flowers. *Notocactus oxycostatus* is an outstanding species, with large, very white areoles around the glossy reddish brown spines. It has bell-shaped yellow flowers. *Notocactus rutilans* is an unusual and choice species. The flowers are large and carmine-coloured, shading to yellow and white in the throat. *Notocactus scopa* var. *candidus* is a lovely, deservedly popular species, which is entirely covered in soft white spines. It has large, canary yellow

and for providing dramatic accent plants in the house and conservatory. The plants come in a surprising variety of size and shape. There are taller-growing species available as slender columns, while tree- and shrub-like species grow by producing a succession of round and oval pads, as in the classic prickly pear varieties. There are also many shrubby, prostrate and creeping forms, however, as well as some stockier upright growers. Although they do flower quite readily, these plants are especially useful for their structure and form. They are guaranteed to create real interest, as most people cannot believe that any cacti, let alone such big ones, will grow happily in their gardens and flower and set seed each year.

ABOVE *Opuntia violacea*, like other plants in this genus, is a great attention-grabber

ABOVE Half-hardy *Opuntia subulata* makes an exotic summer companion to a hardy, all-year-round planting of yuccas and of phormiums

flowers. *Notocactus uebelmannianus* is a very fine-looking, glossy, dark green cactus, with attractive wavy spines which are flattened against the plant and sometimes interlacing. It bears glossy, wine-red flowers.

NAME: **OPUNTIA**

Origin: The Americas and the West Indies
Description: The opuntias are an exception to the leisurely habit of growth among the cacti so this enormous genus is excellent for creating a large presence in your garden bed or planters,

ABOVE *Opuntia robusta* in snow – it will grow outside in mild areas

ABOVE *Opuntia jamaicensis*

Popular species and varieties:
Good for summer/permanent bedding

AY TALL B/S *Opuntia acanthocarpa* has branching cylindrical stems and large red and yellow flowers. It will grow over 6ft (2m) high. *Opuntia basilaris* is a very attractive species with grey-blue pads, fine spines and brown glochids. The pads are often heart shaped. *Opuntia chlorotica* has large bluish green stems on a branching stem which reaches a height of over 6ft (2m). *Opuntia phaeacantha* is a bushy plant with oval pads and yellow flowers. *Opuntia lindheimeri* var. *linguiformis* is a bushy plant. Its large oval pads have only a few spines. It bears large flowers which are predominantly yellow, fading to red. Reaches up to 3ft (1m). *Opuntia spinosior* eventually grows into a tree-like plant with large yellow or purple flowers. *Opuntia violacea* has pretty lilac-tinged grey pads, which are large and oval. It carries attractive large yellow flowers with red throats and reaches over 6ft (2m) tall.

Opuntia violacea var. *macrocentra* has bluish green pads about 5in (12cm) wide and yellow flowers and grows up to 3ft (1m) tall.
SB TALL B/S *Opuntia bergeriana* has spiny, bright green pads, 4–10in (10–25cm) long by 2–4in (5–10 cm) wide, clustering freely. It has readily produced red flowers and it can eventually reach 6–9ft (2–3m) or so in height. *Opuntia cylindrica* is a useful, tall-growing cylindrical plant with large yellow flowers. *Opuntia imbricata* has strongly spined, tall, branching, cylindrical stems with purple and yellow flowers. It grows up to 9ft (3m) tall. *Opuntia subulata* is similar to *Opuntia cylindrica*. It has rapidly growing clustering columns, and it can be made to branch dramatically if you cut it back regularly. It can be trained to arch overhead like a weird, prickly arbour. Eventually it has red flowers, but it does need to be very large before it will bloom.
AY Prostrate forms – MF *Opuntia compressa* is a prostrate plant, forming creeping and spreading clumps of dark green, oval pads up to 4in (10cm) across, and it is easier-to-handle than some opuntias because there are few, if any, spines. It produces large yellow flowers. *Opuntia elata* is another, easier to handle, opuntia, which has smooth, rounded, dark glossy green pads with very few, if any, spines and orange-red flowers. *Opuntia hystricina* is a

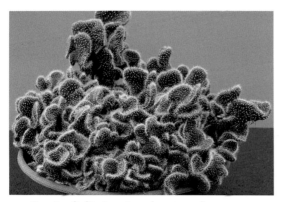

ABOVE *Opuntia cylindrica is a cristate/monstrous plant*

low-growing, clump-forming species with almost circular pads, often flushed pink or purple, and large yellow flowers. *Opuntia macrohiza* grows prostrate, in colonies. It has large bluish green segments with few or no spines, and large yellow flowers with a red centre. *Opuntia polyacantha* is another bushy, prostrate plant with spiny pads and yellow flowers. *Opuntia tortispina* is a scrambling plant with circular or oval pads, white, often twisted, spines and sulphur yellow flowers. *Opuntia tortispina* var. *cymochila* is another prostrate scrambler made up of circular pads about 3in (8cm) across. It has very large yellow flowers.

SB Prostrate forms – MF *Opuntia chaffeyi* is prostrate and freely branching, with long, thin stems issuing from a large, fleshy root. The flowers are lemon yellow. *Opuntia erectoclada* grows with small creeping pads and soon forms a colony. It offers a contrast with its glossy, deep carmine-red flowers.

Good for the house/conservatory
SML/MED B/S Upright forms *Opuntia brasilensis* has fresh green miniature pads and yellow flowers. *Opuntia microdasys* is one you will recognize, with its beautiful flat pads displaying tufts of cream hairs or, in variety, very yellow hairs. This is the renowned bunnies' ears. It isn't as friendly as it sounds,

though, as the tiny spines are incredibly irritating if they get into your fingers. *Opuntia microdasys* var. *albispina* has elegant white tufts of hair on flat, pale green pads. These hairs are soft to the touch and rarely detach themselves into fingers. *Opuntia monacatha variegata* has pale green flattened stems, very attractively marbled with cream and yellow. *Opuntia rufida* has flat pads with attractive red brown areoles. *Opuntia stenopetala* has greyish green pads, and its orange-red flowers are easily produced on quite small specimens. It is a fast-growing species. *Opuntia tuna* is a shrubby, branching plant with bright green pads. Its large yellow and red flowers are readily produced. *Opuntia verschaffeltii* is another cylindrical species and one of the easier opuntias to flower, producing red blooms quite readily. *Opuntia vestita* is an attractive, pale, cylindrical plant, covered with fluffy white hair and excellent for contrasts.
CR/MO These are sculptural and much prized for their twisted shapes. *Opuntia robusta* var. *monstrosus* grows into attractive miniature grey columns with very small, elongated pads. *Opuntia tuna* var. *monstrosus* has clustering small, bright green pads on flattened elongated stems. *Opuntia vestita* var. *cristata* forms prickly, densely hairy undulating forms.

ABOVE **The opuntias are popular 'accent' plants.** *Opuntia subulata,* **seen here, flowers only when it has grown very tall**

ABOVE **The shaggy white 'hair' of the oroecereus genus gives the plants their old man cacti nickname. This is *Oreocereus doelzianus***

NAME: **OREOCEREUS**　　　　TALL CO

Origin: South America
Description: Also named borzicactus, these are known collectively as old man cacti because they have long, shaggy hair and, when grouped in a collection, suggest nothing so much as a gathering of the elderly in a rest home.
Popular species and varieties: *Oreocereus celsianus* is tall-growing and covered in wispy white hair, with almost 4in (9cm) long, dull pink flowers and reaches over 3ft (1m) tall. *Oreocereus doelzianus* has zygomorphic (asymmetrical Christmas cactus-like) flowers, with a bluish red colouring and it grows up to 3ft (1m) tall.

NAME: *PELARGONIUM CARNOSUM*　　SML C

Origin: South Africa
Description: Surely a most unusual member of the geranium-type family, grows into an

interesting 'miniature palm'. It has swollen, branching stems, often twisted or gnarled, up to 2in (5cm) thick. A good bonsai type of plant with numerous whitish flowers.

NAME: **PELECYPHORA (ALSO KNOWN AS STROMBOCACTUS)**　　SML SGL

Origin: Mexico
Description: This genus is prized for its pectinate spines. They have a densely packed, feathery appearance, like the teeth of a comb, and are almost artificial in their perfect symmetry, which makes them both distinctive and desirable.
Popular species and varieties: *Pelecyphora aseliformis* is 2–4in (5–10cm) high with flattened and elongated tubercles. *Pelecyphora pseudopectinatus* var. *rubriflora* is a rare and prized plant which initially has globular stems, later elongating, with numerous short, feathery spines and red flowers. *Pelecyphora* (*Strombocactus*) *valdezianus* is a miniature rarity with hair-like, feathery spines and violet-pink flowers.

NAME: **PERESKIA**　　　　TALL B/S

Origin: The Americas and the West Indies
Description: These plants represent one of the earliest evolutionary stages in the development of the cacti we now see, as they are primitive, leafy and shrub-like, and have areoles with one

RIGHT *Pelecyphora aseliformis*

ABOVE *Pelargonium carnosum*

ABOVE *Pereskia aculeata*

to three spines but no glochids. Large in habitat they can make an interesting container shrub in cultivation.

Popular species and varieties: *Pereskia aculeata* var. *godseffiana* has very pretty peach-coloured leaves and eventually reaches 6–10ft (2–3m) height and 3ft (1m) spread. *Pereskia grandifolia* is useful for a bushy effect. It has rose-like, purple flowers with pear-shaped fruits. In habitat it reaches 15ft (5m), with a spread of 3ft (1m).

NAME: *PORTULACARIA AFRA*   SB MED B/S

Origin: South Africa
Description: With its red stems and angular branches this rapidly makes a small shrub and it can also be pruned into convincing little 'bonsai' trees.

ABOVE *Portulacaria afra* 'Foliisvariegatus'

Popular species and varieties: *Portulacaria afra* has plain green leaves. It is especially useful in its variegated form, *P. afra* 'Foliisvariegatus', with green and yellow leaves, which is a pretty shrub, with red, very branching stems and emerald leaves; it can be pruned into very convincing little trees.

NAME: SCHLUMBERGERA   TR

Origin: South America

Description: Christmas cacti and Easter cacti, known as Holiday cacti in the USA, are popular houseplants and widely available at Christmas and Easter time. Cultivars have been bred in a variety of attractive colours, including pinks, whites and multicolours. Pot two plants back to back for a full container, otherwise the container will look very asymmetrical. They enjoy a slightly shaded position, and a little more water than normal, but do not allow the compost to remain saturated. They enjoy an acid soil, so use ericaceous compost. Keep them above 45°F (7°C) and for whites/gold 55F (12°C) or the cultivars will develop pink flushing. Winter-flowering types need ten hours of darkness to induce bud formation, something

ABOVE *Sedum spectabile* 'Brilliant' (ice plant)

that will occur naturally so long as you keep them out of exposure to strong artificial light overnight. Do not move the plants once they are in bud, or the buds may drop.

Popular species and varieties: *Schlumbergera bridgesii* is the common 'Christmas cactus', with cerise flowers. Look too for *Schlumbergera obtusangula*, a rare species which looks like a miniature prickly pear or opuntia cactus with lilac flowers. Good cultivars include 'Bristol Princess' (RHS award of merit) with a white or very pale pink mid-stripe on the petals, shading to pale lilac; 'Frankenstolz', one of the best old German cultivars, which is scarlet with some lavender; 'Pedca Beauty', a lovely shell-pink and free-flowering; 'Weihnachtsfreude' with orange and pink flowers with some magenta. There is also 'Delicatus', which is white, sometimes with touch of pink, and 'Gold Charm', an unusual and attractive warm gold flower, but unfortunately a much less vigorous grower than many of the other cultivars. It needs warmth, or a pink flushing will appear giving it a nasty, muddy colour.

ABOVE *Schlumbergera* 'Bristol Rose'

Easter cactus, as the name suggests, have a later flowering cycle than the Christmas cacti, but in all other respects they are largely the same. *Schlumbergera gaertneri* (syn. *Rhipsalis gaertneri*), the Easter cactus, has large vermillion flowers; *Rhipsalidopsis rosea* is a miniature plant with deep pink to lilac flowers. Cultivars include 'Elektra' with large, lilac flowers and 'Scarborough', which is a deep maroon colour with an unusual yellow throat.

NAME: SEDUM

Origin: Wide distribution in the northern hemisphere and South America

Description: Sedums are reminiscent of the crassulas in their variety of form. The hardy perennial mat-forming sedums are ideal for carpeting and pond edging, etc. Trailing sedums are lovely plants for strawberry pots or hanging containers, and they can also be grown along the length of a trough at the top of a wall to produce a magnificent curtain.

Popular species and varieties:

AY MF *Sedum acre* 'Yellow Queen' is an evergreen, mat-forming perennial. It has dense spreading shoots, clothed in tiny, fleshy, pale green leaves that are variegated yellow; plus abundant small yellow flowers. It grows to 1–2in (2.5–5cm) high with indefinite spread. *Sedum album* is a well-known, succulent perennial. Very vigorous and quite variable, depending on whether it's grown in a drought-ridden position on a wall or more lushly in the ground. Leaves are small and blunt-ended, ranging from red to brown in dry conditions through to green. Grows to 2in (5cm) tall with an indefinite spread. *Sedum album* f. *murale* 'Coral Carpet' is a hardy succulent perennial. This colourful cultivar has small, rounded or cylindrical leaves, bright red and maroon in the sun, and small white flowers. It grows to 2in (5cm) tall with an indefinite spread. *Sedum ellacombianum* is a hardy succulent perennial, bright green with toothed leaves and yellow

ABOVE *Sedum middendorffianum*

flowers. It grows to 1½in (4cm) high with an indefinite spread. *Sedum middendorffianum* is a hardy succulent perennial. This is another mat-forming species, with green-brown leaves and striking yellow-orange spiky flowers. It has a variable height from 1½in (4cm) with an indefinite spread. *Sedum spathulifolium* var. *purpureum* is a hardy succulent perennial. It has flat rosettes of fleshy grey and purple leaves and clusters of small yellow flowers. It grows to 1½in (4cm) high and has an indefinite spread. *Sedum spathulifolium* 'Cape Blanco' is a hardy succulent perennial. This is another sedum perfect for dramatic carpet bedding. Flat rosettes of fleshy, silvery leaves give another useful colour contrast. Also has clusters of small yellow flowers. It grows from 1½in (4cm) high and has an indefinite spread. **TR** Donkeys' tails are some of the nicest and funniest succulent plants you can grow. They produce long, pendant 'tails', with overlapping leaves, like scales, giving the whole plant a really textured finish. *Sedum morganianum* is a larger version. It is a beautiful grey succulent trailing plant which makes a wonderful cascade in a strawberry pot or spilling out of the neck of a classical urn. *Sedum*

ABOVE **Sedum spathulifolium**

morganianum x *Echeveria derenbergii* is a choice hybrid. The echeveria part of its parentage gives the plant altogether larger, chunkier and more open 'tails', with cascades of succulent grey leaves terminating in clumps of yellowish flowers. *Sedum lineare* 'Variegatum' is a mat-forming variegated plant with small narrow leaves, forming a pale green cloud. Good for hanging basket use. *Sedum rubrum* is another colourful choice, with prostrate stems of grey-red succulent leaves. It has white flowers. *Sedum sieboldii* is a really useful plant with delicate, arching stems up to 10in (25cm) long, bearing round turquoise-blue leaves and pink flowers. *Sedum sieboldii* f. *variegatum* has arching stems with variegated cream and grey leaves and pink flowers. **SML B/S** The following are good species for flower. *Sedum cauticola* 'Lidakense' is a compact succulent, with tiny grey-green succulent leaves. It bears rich, dark red flowers. *Sedum frutescens* is an ideal miniature bonsai specimen, developing an impressive trunk. The stems develop a papery bark-like skin, which peels a little like the bark on silver birches, and branches bearing emerald green leaves, but it is also very good for its profuse white flowers. **AY MED B/S** The two following sedum species are often grown as garden plants, when they are cut down in the winter, but they will also look good indoors. *Sedum spectabile*, commonly known as

ABOVE **Sedum pachyclados**

the ice plant, has large, flat-topped pink-purple flower heads in the autumn. It has a height and spread of 18in (45cm) and has many cultivars, which could go together into a fabulous and colourful mixed display. Look for, among others, 'Brilliant', with its bright pink heads, white-flowered 'Snow Queen' and 'Stardust', and dark purple 'Carmen' and 'Meteor'. They are easy to propagate by dividing the root stock, or by taking cuttings in the spring. *Sedum telephium* 'Autumn Joy' has fabulous heads of purple flowers in the autumn. Leave the flowers on, because they produce attractive rust-coloured fruits in early winter, which are long-lasting and are also useful for flower arranging.

ABOVE *Sempervivum tectorum*

NAME: **SEMPERVIVUMS**	AY SML RF

Origin: Mountainous areas of Europe and Asia
Description: These houseleeks grow in symmetrical rosettes of fleshy leaves up to 2½in (6cm) in diameter with a spread of 4in (10cm) upwards. They form hardy ground-hugging mats. They have star-shaped flowers on succulent stems and although the rosettes die after flowering they are replaced by numerous offsets. They are suitable for rock gardens, screes, walls, banks, container gardens and alpine houses.

Popular species and varieties: *Sempervivum arachnoideum* (cobweb houseleek) is a hardy succulent perennial. Evergreen, vigorous and mat-forming, with numerous small green rosettes with a fine 'cobweb' of white hairs joining the leaf tips. *Sempervivum calcareum* is an attractive species with grey-green leaves with purple tips and pink flowers. *Sempervivum tectorum* is a very variable species, with shades of green and

ABOVE *Sempervivum calcareum*

ABOVE *Sempervivum arachnoideum*

brown with or without contrasting tips. It grows to 2–5in (5–12cm) tall. It has rosettes that are 1in (2.5cm) in diameter upwards and it has a spread of 4in (10cm) upwards. Colourful cultivars have been bred, such as 'Caramel', a delicious warm caramel colour – almost appetizing – along with reds, pinks, bronzes and greys.

NAME: **SENECIO**

Origin: Worldwide distribution, including succulent species from South Africa
Description: Senecio is a huge and globally distributed genus which includes over 1000 species from all over the world. Some are weeds and others are garden plants, but there

ABOVE *Stapelia flavopurpurea* is good on the eye, but its flowers carry a stench

are also a number of succulents from South Africa, including some very covetable species as follows.

Popular species and varieties:
TR Trailing string of beads plants are great fun. They make a dramatic trailing plant which lives up to its name – in time you can have a hanging basket with yards of trailing 'beads'. The plants thrive in slight shade, and they will benefit from plenty of water and feeding in the growing season, when they will fatten up into satisfying round beads – like children's 'popper beads' of years ago, or nice fat garden peas straight from the pod, so watch out for your children! *Senecio herreanus* has green, slightly elliptical, bead-like leaves, which are marked with translucent lines, and it has white flowers. *Senecio rowleyanus* is the classic string of beads with bright green bead-like leaves.
MED B/S *Senecio articulatus* is known as the candle plant, because of its pale, finger-thick,

LEFT *Senecio rowleyanus* (string of beads)

jointed stems, which are grey or green with red or brown markings. The plant grows up to 28in (70cm) high, and it will develop heads of delicate leaves if it is given sufficient water. It has yellow flowers. *Senecio coccineiflorus* has elongated rosettes of purple-grey leaves on a trunk-like stem and heads of scarlet flowers. *Senecio haworthii* reaches 12in (30cm) high, with silvery grey-green 2in (5cm) long leaves which grow In spirals, and orange or yellow flowers.

NAME: **STAPELIA**   SML MED SGL

Origin: South Africa

Description: These plants are interesting for two rather opposing qualities. The plants are striking, as thickened succulent plants, with a variety of finger-like forms, and the flowers are truly spectacular, huge and fleshy, often shaped like fat starfish and coloured in maroon, beige, yellow and brown, with blotched and splashed markings. So far so good. Unfortunately the smell of the flowers is far from fragrant: as they are pollinated by flies that are tricked into seeing the blooms as carrion, they carry the pungent odour of death. This is, therefore, definitely not one for the house when in flower! Some species are undergoing changes of name, but the following are in common use.

Popular species and varieties: *Stapelia ambigua* has huge star-shaped hairy flowers. *Stapelia asterias* var. *lucida* has glossy purple-brown flowers. *Stapelia flavirostris* is a vigorous plant which has very large, purple, star-shaped, hairy flowers with wavy yellow lines. *Stapelia flavopurpurea* has yellow and red flowers. *Stapelia gigantea* has huge red and yellow flowers. *Stapelia margarita* (also know as *S. hirsuta*) has dramatic, star-shaped flowers, dull red with yellowish wrinkles, and a dense cushion of reddish hairs. *Stapelia variegata* has beautiful star-shaped yellow and purple flowers which have to be seen to be believed.

NAME: **SULCOREBUTIA**   SML SGL

Origin: South America

Description: These plants are globular and generally clump-forming. They are collected for their interesting spines and for their numerous large flowers, which come in a variety of vivid, glossy colours, almost fluorescent in their intensity. Like most of the flowering cacti, these plants grow well from seed.

Popular species and varieties: *Sulcorebutia candiae* has large deep yellow flowers. *Sulcorebutia crispata* is a grey-green plant with white to red-brown spines which are curved and curling into the stem. It has large and stunning dark magenta flowers. *Sulcorebutia frankiana* is an olive-green plant with large, glossy maroon flowers. *Sulcorebutia menesesii*

ABOVE *Sulcorebutia menesesii*

ABOVE *Trichocereus candicans*

ABOVE *Thelocactus bicolor*

is a choice plant, with attractive curly spines and golden yellow flowers. *Sulcorebutia mentosa* has shiny dark green stems which produce numerous rich purple flowers. *Sulcorebutia tiraquensis* var. *electracantha* is a clumping species covered in white spines, with orange to red flowers. *Sulcorebutia vasqueziana* has an unusual blackish green to violet-black body, with weak, tangled golden-yellow to reddish spines. The flowers are pretty, in magenta or red, and yellow inside.

NAME: **THELOCACTUS**	SML SGL

Origin: The Americas
Description: These are small, globular plants, often with interesting spination. They are free-flowering, in a range of colours including white, pink, red, yellow and lilac, with glossy

petals. Some have an almost continuous stream of flowers from the late spring onwards.

Popular species and varieties: *Thelocactus bicolor* has attractively coloured spines, in contrasting red and brown, and large, deep pink flowers. *Thelocactus setispinus* has a strongly ribbed body and yellow flowers produced in sequence from summer through to the autumn. *Thelocactus tulensis* is a dramatic brown plant with long grey spines. The magnificent white flowers have a pretty pink midstripe.

NAME: **TITANOPSIS**	SML SGL

Origin: South Africa

Description: This is another really interesting genus, in which mimicry is taken to great heights. The plants have encrusted leaves, with a greyish white textured finish, to camouflage them among the glittering quartz rocks of their habitat.

Popular species and varieties: *Titanopsis fulleri* has rock-like, bluish green leaves on short stems, forming mats. It has dark yellow flowers. *Titanopsis calcarea* has encrusted blue-grey leaves and golden yellow flowers. *Titanopsis luederitzii* has grey leaves with 'rocky' areas at the tips and yellow flowers.

NAME: **TRICHOCEREUS**	SB TALL CO

Origin: South America

Description: This is a columnar-growing genus that is large to tree-like with big funnel-shaped flowers, diurnal, scented and often white. Easy to root from cuttings and offsets, and often used as grafting stock.

Popular species and varieties: *Trichocereus candicans* is a branching, tall-growing 'cowboy'-type cactus, bearing large, 8in (20cm) long, strongly perfumed, white flowers. *Trichocereus litoralis* has white flowers almost 6in (14cm) long by 4in (10cm) in diameter which, unusually, stay open for up to five days. Erect and columnar, it can arch under its own weight, new growth

ABOVE **Titanopsis**

from this becoming vertical again. *Trichocereus spachiana* forms tall, dark green columns which are freely branching. It has very impressive blooms, which grow up to 8in (20cm) long by 6in (15cm) wide, with white inner petals and greenish tinged outer petals.

NAME: **TURBINICARPUS**	SML SGL

Origin: The Americas

Description: These are choice, small-growing plants with blue-green or grey-green stems and

ABOVE *Turbinicarpus schmiedickeanus* var. *macrochele*

147

ABOVE *Yucca gloriosa* 'Variegata' in flower on the left, alongside half-hardy *Agave americana* 'Variegata'

papery, curved spines. They are covetable little gems, which also have the bonus of producing relatively large flowers for such tiny plants.

Popular species and varieties: *Turbinocarpus schmiedickeanus* is a choice miniature, up to 1in (2.5cm) across and covered in broad papery spines. It has white or pink flowers. *Turbinicarpus schmiedickeanus* var. *klinkerianus* is an attractive grey plant with cream flowers which are regularly produced in the spring. *Turbinicarpus schmiedickeanus* var. *macrochele* is a good-looking plant with tangled spines

and white flowers, suffused with pink. The spines are long and grey, curving inwards like flat, flexible hooks. *Turbinicarpus schmiedickeanus* var. *schwarzii* is a grey-green plant, its cream flowers having a pale pink central stripe on each petal. It has soft, grey, curved spines, very few in number.

NAME: YUCCA   **TALL RF**

Origin: The Americas and the West Indies
Description: Spiky and architectural, hardy yuccas are ideal garden subjects for a high-

impact scheme. Their tall, long-lasting panicles of creamy flowers are carried in the summer.

Popular species and varieties:

AY *Yucca filamentosa* 'Bright Edge' is a stemless and rosette-forming perennial evergreen, with variegated leaves, deep green with narrow yellow margins, which fray attractively at the edges, producing curly white threads. It readily produces panicles of white flowers, 3–6ft (1–2m) tall, in the summer, and it reaches 6ft (2m) tall and 5ft (1.5m) spread. *Yucca flaccida* 'Variegata' is another stemless, rosette-forming perennial evergreen, with softly drooping variegated leaves, green with bright margins and a height and spread of 5ft (1.5m). Its flower panicle is 1½–3ft (45cm–1m) or so tall with creamy white flowers. *Yucca gloriosa* 'Variegata' is very showy and a hardy alternative to *Agave americana* 'Variegata', reaching 9 x 9ft (3 x 3m) eventually. This species forms a trunk, topped with a rosette of stiff, sword-like pointed leaves, green with yellow edges with age, but variegated yellow, green and pink in small specimens. It carries white flower panicles.

ABOVE *Yucca elephantipes*

SB *Yucca elephantipes* is a common houseplant, but as it belongs to the Agavaceae it sneaks in here as a really useful, quick-growing succulent. Most yuccas are fully hardy, and even this one will survive in milder areas in the garden. In the conservatory it will soon grow into a significantly sized shrub or a small tree, making an exotic and architectural impact, especially with its distinctive multiple trunks that form near the ground. It has long, narrow, pointed leaves, which are rather leathery, and larger plants will produce very attractive panicles of pendant, tulip-shaped flowers in the summer months. *Yucca elephantipes* 'Variegata' is a useful, more colourful cultivar. It is striped with white margins to the edges of the leaves.

ABOVE **The bold rosette of *Yucca filamentosa* 'Bright Edge' makes a strong focal point in this raised bed**

Glossary

Accent planting a particularly large and dramatic plant or plants, used as the most important feature in a scheme

Acid soil soil that has a pH value of less than 7

Alpines strictly speaking plants that have originated in the high mountains, above the tree line, but used as a loose general term for all rockery plants

Annuals plants that complete their whole life cycle in one year

Areole of cacti, the portion of the plant from which the spines originate

Architectural in the sense of plants, refers to plants that have a particularly strong shape and form

Basal rosette leaves radiating from a central point at ground level

Biennial plants that complete their whole life cycle from germination, flowering and seeding to death in two years; producing roots, stems and leaves in the first year, and flowering, seeding and dying in the second year

Bloom a blue or greyish fine, waxy or powdery coating on leaves or stems

Bonsai-like succulents tree-like succulents, which make instant or almost instant, miniature trees for growing in pots

Borderline hardy will survive in an average to warmer than average British winter, but which will be cut down by severe and prolonged frosts

Bract a modified leaf, which is produced at the base of a flower, or a flower cluster. They are often large and brightly coloured

Candelabrum (of plants) a plant with a number of branching arms

Carpet bedding low-growing, mat-forming and often succulent plants which can be used in a tapestry-effect planting scheme

Carpeting succulents succulents suitable for use in carpet bedding schemes

Caudex the swollen base of stem or root of a succulent plant, adapted as a water-storage organ

Caudiciform a plant which forms a caudex

Chlorophyll the green pigment in plant leaves and stems which absorbs energy from sunlight

CITES the Convention on International Trade in Endangered Species of Wild Fauna and Flora. These regulations have been designed to prohibit the removal of endangered species from their natural habitat, and to control the trade in these species. The members of the family cactaceae involved are listed in Appendix 1 of CITES

Cleft graft see grafting, scion, stock: a form of graft designed for relatively flat scions, in which the scion is inserted and fastened down into a central slit which has been cut into the surface of the stock

Continental climate characterized by the hot summers, cold winters and low rainfall typical of conditions in the interior of a continent away from the sea

Cristate a deformed plant, where the growing point has developed an abnormal crested or twisted form

Cultivar an artificially produced plant, either bred or selected, which can be propagated while retaining its characteristics

Deciduous describes plants that produce fresh leaves annually at the beginning of the growing season, and then lose them when the growing season comes to an end

Desiccated dehydrated and dried up

Diagonal graft see grafting, scion, stock: a form of graft designed for slender scions, in which the surfaces of the scion and the stock are joined with slanting, diagonal cuts to give the maximum area of contact between them

Dormancy a period of low or absent plant growth, usually associated with low winter temperatures and light levels

Ericaceous (of compost) acidic, and therefore suitable for acid-loving plants

Felt see bloom

Flat grafting see grafting, scion, stock: the 'normal' form of graft, where the scion and stock are joined together at horizontally cut surfaces

Frost pocket a purely localized area, which, because of geographical features, is significantly colder in winter than the surrounding areas

Fully hardy a plant which can tolerate temperatures of down to 5°F (−15°C)

Genus a group of species that share enough common characteristics to be grouped together for the purpose of botanical identification

Globular (of plants) having a spherical or ball-like shape

Grafting a method of propagation by which a rare, slow-growing or difficult-to-cultivate plant is removed from its own roots (thus becoming the scion) and artificially attached to a more vigorous, rooted parent plant (the stock)

Ground cover carpeting and mat-forming species that rapidly cover bare areas

Half hardy plants which can only go outside after any danger of frost has passed and which have to come indoors for the winter before frosts are likely

Hardy describes the resilience of plant to cold, subdivided into frost hardy: able to withstand temperatures down to (23°F) (−5°C)

Hard core material, such as broken bricks and rocks, which acts as a compacted foundation layer for a surface material such as gravel or paving slabs

Hard landscaping structures in the garden such as paths, steps, patios, etc.

Hardiness zones see Harvard University hardiness zones

Harvard University hardiness zones a system developed in the USA at Harvard University in which areas are rated according to the temperature requirements of the plants that they can support

Herbaceous plants which die down at the end of the growing season

Hybrid offspring of at least two different species or varieties of plant, which can be naturally or artificially produced

In-filling temporary planting to fill in a bed or border until the permanent planting matures sufficiently to fill the space

Inflorescence a flowering shoot, which carries more than one flower

Invasive plants which can quickly outgrow their space and/or overwhelm their neighbours

Knot garden a formal garden, comprising regular beds planted on a geometrical pattern, divided by low hedging, such as box (*Buxus sempervirens*)

Marginal a moisture-loving species, which enjoys a damp position on the edges of a pond or other water feature

Maritime climate a climate affected by proximity to the sea, which results in a relatively small temperature difference between the summer and winter months and fairly high rainfall

Microclimate a climate that is particular to a very small area and affected by local factors, e.g. the higher temperatures found in a city environment because of the combination of shelter created by buildings and the extra heat resulting from the escape of energy from densely packed habitation, industry, etc.

Mid-stripe a central band of contrasting colour in a leaf or flower petal

Mulch a layer of material added to the soil surface to protect plants, suppress weeds and retain moisture

Non-invasive a plant that will not outgrow its position or affect neighbouring plants

Offsetting a plant which produces miniature replicas of itself, usually around its base

Panicle a branched flower cluster

Permeable membrane this is a layer of material designed to be placed between the surface of the soil and a top dressing of gravel; it suppresses weeds and light while allowing air and water to pass through it

Pricking out transplanting seedlings or young plants which are becoming crowded into another container to give them more space to grow

Propagate to produce extra plants by setting seeds, taking cuttings, grafting, etc.

Prostrate a sprawling, low-growing habit

Ribs a feature of some cacti, which have their surface divided into raised sections bearing areoles

Rosette-shaped a group of leaves which radiate from a central point

Scion see grafting, stock, vascular tissue: the part of a rare, slow-growing or difficult-to-cultivate plant which has been removed from its own roots and artificially attached to a more vigorous-rooted parent plant

Sour soil soil that has become starved of nutrients or has an undesirable build-up of chemicals

Species a member of a genus

Spines/spination a hard outgrowth from a stem; in cacti they are an evolutionary modification of leaves

Stock see grafting, scion, vascular tissue: a vigorous plant, with its top section removed to be replaced by an artificially attached rootless section of a rare, slow-growing or difficult-to-cultivate plant, which will grow more successfully with the support of the host plant's root sytem

Subspecies members of a species, which share common features within themselves that separate them from the rest of the species

Succulent/ence (of plants) a plant that has evolved to withstand periods of drought, by modifying the leaves, stems or roots for improved water storage

Summer bedding see half hardy

Systemic insecticide a longer-lasting chemical taken up into the whole of the plant so that it continues to poison insects which feed on it; as opposed to a non-systemic insecticide, which coats the outside of the plant and insects temporarily but is soon washed away

Temperate climate/zone a moderate or mild climate; areas which have such a climate

Topiary trees or bushes, which have been trained and clipped into artificial shapes e.g. geometrical or animal shapes

Trailing a plant with long stems which hang down; particularly useful for baskets, window boxes, etc.

Tubercles small, warty protuberances

Variegation foliage that displays lighter banding, striping or spotting

Vascular tissue a slightly darker core in the centre of a stem, surrounded by a circle of cells which act as water-storing tissue. For a graft to be successful, the vascular tissue of the stock and scion has to be in contact in at least one place

Vegetative propagation the increase of plants by cuttings, grafts or removing offsets, as opposed to raising plants from seed

Vestigial simple in structure, with reduced size and function

Water table the point at which you reach the water-saturated layer under the surface of the soil

Winter protection a layer of protective material, such as horticultural fleece, sacking, straw or even the plant's own foliage, which is used to cover the plant over the winter. The protected plant can then stay outside happily all winter

Woody (stems) a persistent stem of woody fibres, which means that the plant does not die down over the winter as herbaceous material does

About the author

Since 1977 Shirley-Anne has been running Glenhirst Cactus Nursery in Lincolnshire, east England, a retail, mail-order and Internet-based plant business, with her husband Neville. Over the past 12 years or so they have become increasingly interested in growing hardy and half-hardy cacti and other succulents in the garden, along with exotic and Mediterranean plants such as palms and olives. Shirley-Anne has also designed and, with Neville, planted up a number of exotic/Mediterranean-style gardens in Lincolnshire, and they have created their own garden together at the Nursery.

The couple travels around the East Midlands, England, giving talks to gardening clubs, plant societies and other groups on 'Design with Cacti and Succulents', 'Mediterranean-style Gardening in the UK' and 'A Crash Course in Garden History', plus talks on garden tourism, including places to visit and what to look for. The talks include slides, quizzes and demonstrations, and are designed to be light-hearted and entertaining as well as informative.

They are also enthusiastic photographers, travelling all over the UK and Europe photographing plants and gardens for books, magazine articles and the GardenWorld Images (formerly Harry Smith Collection) photo library. They also enjoy their work as wedding and portrait photographers.

Shirley-Anne has written numerous articles on gardening and garden tourism for magazines, plus three previous books for

GMC: *Success with Mediterranean Gardens, Growing Cacti and Other Succulents in the Conservatory and Indoors* and *Growing Cacti and Other Succulents in the Garden.*

Shirley-Anne can be contacted at:
Glenhirst Cactus Nursery,
Station Road,
Swineshead,
Boston,
Lincs. PE20 3NX, UK.
Tel: +44 (0)1205 820314
Fax: +44 (0)1205 820614
E-mail: info@cacti4u.co.uk
Web: http://www.cacti4u.co.uk

Index

Pages highlighted in **bold** include illustrations of plants

GMC Publications
Castle Place, 166 High Street, Lewes, East Sussex BN7 1XU, United Kingdom
Tel: 01273 488005 Fax: 01273 402866
E-mail: pubs@thegmcgroup.com Website: www.gmcbooks.com
Contact us for a complete catalogue, or visit our website. Orders by credit card are accepted.